MYSTERY OF AMERICA: BOOK 1
ENIGMATIC MYSTERIES
AND
ANOMALOUS ARTIFACTS
OF NORTH AMERICA:

A CONNECTION TO
THE ANCIENT PAST

Tédd St. Rain

Tim,
THanks for
Your support

LOST ARTS MEDIA
LONG BEACH, CA

MYSTERY OF AMERICA: BOOK 1 – ENIGMATIC MYSTERIES AND ANOMALOUS ARTIFACTS OF NORTH AMERICA: A CONNECTION TO THE ANCIENT PAST

ISBN 1-59016-999-9

ALSO AVAILABLE ON AUDIO BOOK, VIDEO TAPE AND DVD (see Page 77)

CONCEPT, RESEARCH, LAYOUT AND DESIGN
Tédd St. Rain

BACKGROUND COVER ART BY DOUGLAS TAYLOR • WWW.SOULICJOURNEYS.COM

Table of Contents

MYSTERY OF AMERICA: BOOK 1
ENIGMATIC MYSTERIES AND ANOMALOUS ARTIFACTS OF NORTH AMERICA: A CONNECTION TO THE ANCIENT PAST

Presented by Tédd St. Rain

The exact contrary
of what is generally
believed is often the truth.

–Jean de la Bruyere

INTRODUCTION

There are many people today who take a great interest in our past and our history as a civilization. The planet on which we live has a number of mysterious and often enigmatic remnants and artifacts that continue to baffle many scientists and archaeologists. There is a recurring theme that many of the ancient relics have in common, that of being of such unwieldy proportions or sophistication, it is hard to believe that primitive human hands alone could have fashioned them. What we do know of the first recorded civilizations indicates they had a high degree of sophistication (even by today's standards) in many of the fledging arts and sciences we take for granted. These include the development of and expertise in agriculture, writing, mathematics, cosmology, weights and measures, contracts, education, justice, time reckoning, the Zodiac, art, metallurgy, sculpture and painting, amongst many others.

World Map
Babylonia 600 B.C.E.

Modern-day research and scholarship have revealed some interesting details of these ancient civilizations that may explain the nearly instantaneous rise of civilization nearly 6,000

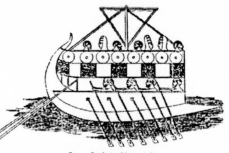

**Sea-Going Vessel
Assyrian Relief 800 B.C.E.**

years ago (See Sitchin, Freer, Gardner and others in the bibliography). There is mounting evidence that an extraterrestrial influence may have shaped mankind's early history and may even be responsible for our very existence.

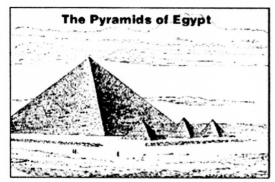

The Pyramids of Egypt

When one considers ancient mysteries of the world what frequently comes to mind are romantic images of the pyramids of Egypt and Mexico, the crumbling walls of Babylon, and of Greece and Rome, the ruins of Baalbek, the remnants of a lost civilization in the Andes, and many others. People travel all over the world to visit places such as these, and yet some of the most perplexing, enigmatic and profound artifacts and structures have been found right here in North America. It is unfortunate that few people outside of certain circles have heard of these incredible archaeological finds. This book (and companion lecture on Video and DVD) will present evidence supporting the notion that there may have been "others" who have come before us. "Others" who have either left, died out, or have returned from elsewhere, possibly as the modern UFO phenomenon.

DEEP WITHIN THE ARCHIVES

A large mountain of evidence available from literary and other sources is available to support the hypothesis that something strange has occurred in the remote past on this planet. Unfortunately, most of the so-called "reputable" institutions have been more interested in piecing together mankind's historical record than in understanding the significance of the rare and unusual artifacts that from time to time come to their attention. Of much greater concern is the methodical and systematic way in which the authorities and powers-that-be have hidden the truth, oftentimes suppressing evidence that would revise the early history of America, and in many notable cases would completely rewrite the record, and mankind's place in it, on this planet.

The legendary Vatican archives are an excellent example. There is no doubt that the libraries and storehouses on and below the grounds of the less-than-a-square-mile sovereign republic known as Vatican City contain a wealth of information about mankind's past. The Vatican library is renowned the world over for its extensive collection on every subject conceivable. There are even rumors of hidden passageways and secret vaults used as safe storage for some of the most incredible curios imaginable. After two millennia of acquisitions, in all likelihood the most unusual of the unusual lie within its walls, literally containing the "secrets of the ages." Astounding artifacts which, if were made public, would revise our understanding and shine the torch of illumination on the complicated history of both the old and new worlds.

The archives of the Smithsonian Institution certainly rival those of the Vatican, in quantity, if not in depth and scope. The Smithsonian Institution was created when its namesake, British scientist James Smithson, bequeathed that his estate should go "to the United States of America, to found at Washington, under the name of the Smithsonian Institution, an establishment for the increase and diffusion of knowledge among men." The motives behind Smithson's bequest remain mysterious. He never traveled to the United States and seems to have had no correspondence with anyone here.

It should come as no surprise as to how many of the objects described in the literature and acquired by the Smithsonian have become "lost" or "unaccounted for." Many times they acknowledge having received an object, but its present location is unknown, or there is some other problem, as in a notable case from the Crumf Burial Cave. In 1892, there were several wood coffins that had been hollowed out by fire, aided by stone or copper chisels, discovered in a cave near Birmingham, Alabama. Eight of these coffins were reportedly taken to the Smithsonian, which in the 1950s claimed they had "not been able to find the specimens in our collection, though records show that they were received." Later, in 1992, the Smithsonian told the President of the Gungywamp Society, David Barron, that the coffins could not be viewed because they were housed in an asbestos-contaminated warehouse that would be closed for the next ten years, and which no one was allowed into except Smithsonian personnel. It would be interesting to know where the coffins are now.

Over the past nearly couple hundred years the Smithsonian has played a part in many of the archaeological finds in North America, sometimes accepting material after no one else knew what to do with it. As a result they have collected over a million artifacts, only a small number of which are available for public viewing. Because of this involvement, they have become the main storehouse for many of the obscure and hard-to-explain rarities uncovered on American soil. In addition to the Smithsonian, many colleges and universities, among them the University of Pennsylvania, University of Chicago and the University of California, were involved and thus claimed the booty, from many of the 19th and 20th century discoveries. Amongst these various archives, institutions, and museums, open only to a select few, lie human-like remains dug up over the past several centuries. Within the literature exists reference to many of these finds, a number of which refer to burials of humans that would be considered giants by today's standards. While many of these interments were the result of "mound builder" activity, primarily from the Adena, Hopewell and Mississippian cultures, there have been several notable exceptions where the remains most likely predate any historical habitation in the area.

THERE WERE GIANTS ON THE EARTH

There have been a number of modern-day giants, such as the Swans, a happily-married giant couple from around the turn of the century. What concerns us most, however, is any number of enigmatic oversized skeletons unearthed in America.

The Swan Giants
Circa 1900

In a classic example of mound builder activity, an article[1] reports that near Brewersville, Indiana, a stone mound more than 70 feet in diameter was excavated, in 1879, which contained skeletons, at least one of which was over nine and half feet tall. At its feet was a human image of burned clay embedded with pieces of flint. Weapons that had been buried nearby were not common to Native Americans in the area. The excavation was supervised by Indiana State archaeologists, and others from the neighborhood states of New York and Ohio. In an affirmation to the lackadaisical attitude of such discoveries in the past, the artifacts were kept in a basket near the Robinson family grain mill, on whose property they had been found. Unfortunately, in 1937 a flood swept the mill away and with it the contents of the basket, which has never been seen since.

Some of the other "giants" which have been found in North America are much more problematic. There are many burials where the nature and characteristics of the burial indicate the skeletal remains are of an uncommonly old age. Take for instance the discovery in a small now-abandoned town southeast of Tucson, Arizona, called Crittenden. According to newspaper accounts[2] at the time, there was an astounding discovery which, if it is true, could entirely reshape how we view our past. In 1891, while workmen were digging a basement for a commercial building they made a startling discovery. About eight feet below the surface they discovered a large clay-stone sarcophagus. The contractor then called in expert help, and when they opened it they found a granite mummy case which once held the body of a human-like being more than

---

[1]"Remains of Vanished Giants Found in State," *Indianapolis News*, 10 Nov 1975.
[2]*Deseret Weekly*, Salt Lake City, 14 Mar 1891.

twelve feet tall. The mummy had worn long hair and a bird-shaped headdress, possibly of an Egyptian motif. Apparently the body had been buried for so many thousands of years that the bones had turned to dust, but inscriptions on the outside of the mummy case indicate that the being had six toes. We must all take reports like this, as we do everything in life, with a grain of salt. Keeping in mind that some of the less scrupulous newspapers of the day would think up stories such as this to fill out the columns. The fact that the alleged discovery it is not an isolated one, and that similar finds can be found throughout North America, does seem to support this report.

THE LOVELOCK GIANTS

Another famous discovery of oversized human remains was first reported[3] in 1911, when miners harvesting bat guano at Lovelock Cave (about 80 miles northeast of Reno, Nevada) discovered the skeleton of a large mummified human skeleton. The unusual thing about this

Lovelock Skull on Display

particular find, besides its excessive height and the extraordinarily large human skulls, was the fact that the remains showed evidence of red hair and was unlike any Indian known to have lived in North America.

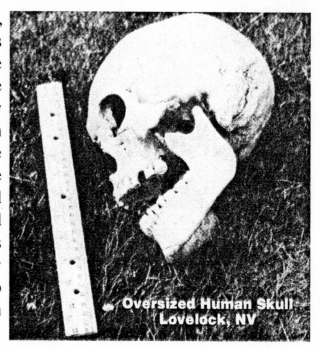

Oversized Human Skull Lovelock, NV

As the workers continued mining past the four-foot level, they continued to discover mummies. A mining engineer and amateur archaeologist, John T. Reid, immediately reported the discovery to numerous colleges and institutions, including the University of Pennsylvania and the Smithsonian Institution. He offered them the opportunity to examine the artifacts as they were being removed from the screens of the mining equipment. Unfortunately, it was over a year before the University of California sent a "non-professional observer," by which time the miners had all but disposed of nearly all the bones and other related artifacts.

Another "observer" who had come later from New York, had accompanied the first man in his observation of the site. What became especially puzzling was that these

3."Nevada's Red-Headed People Eaters," *INFO Journal* (International Fortean Organization, College Park, MD), no. 8, Winter-Spring 1972, pp. 28-29. Also Dorothy P Dansie, "John T. Reid's Case for the Redheaded Giants," *Nevada Historical Society Quarterly*, Fall 1975, pp. 153-167. Also Jim Brandon, Weird America, E.P. Dutton, NY, 1978, pp 131-132.

**Skull Discovery
Lovelock, NV**

men went out of their way to avoid examination of the bones, and at one point, even insisted on the reburial of a complete skeleton that had just been unearthed. Instead, they focused their investigation primarily on pottery shards, fragments of basketry, and the like. It is no surprise that it took 17 years, in 1929, before their findings were published, and then, only in a small article from California. Understandably, Reid became disillusioned with the establishment, and began to document the discoveries as best he could. Many of the testimonials he collected, as well as his personal memoirs, and some baskets and beads from the area can be found in the Nevada State Historical Society library and museum at 1650 North Virginia Street, Reno, NV 89503.

After the refusal of "establishment science" to make a serious investigation into the matter, local Lovelock residents set up makeshift exhibits of the more impressive finds. As has been the case many times with priceless relics of our past, a devastating fire at one of these displays ended up destroying much of what remained.

There have been reports of other oversize skeletons turning up in the area. Skeletons were found in February and June of 1931 in the Humboldt lake bed near the cave. One of these was said to have been wrapped in an Egyptian-like gum-covered material and was about eight and a half feet tall, while another, stood nearly ten feet tall. Another report in the 29 Sep 1939 *Review Miner* tells of a seven-foot-seven-inch skeleton that was found on the Friedman Ranch in the vicinity. As a result of the long series of battles that took place in the area, there may still be quite a few undiscovered finds that would be superficially buried, especially in the area of Carson sink, specifically around the south shore and near Pelican Island. Also, a few miles southwest of Lovelock along the railroad, near Perth, is a gravel pit that has yielded artifacts and mummies. Local Indians claim that artifacts have been found in caves near the Pyramid Lake Reservation about 55 miles to the west.

According to Reid, Indians had told him of petrified giants they had found lying in the open wilderness area to the south of Lovelock Cave. In fact, the local Piute Indians spoke of a race of red-headed giants and the bloody conflict that their forefathers had pursued against them. So ferocious was the Piute abomination toward these Si-Te-Cahs, or "lanky redheads," that a collective crusade to wipe them out was organized by local tribes that were normally at odds with one another. A book published in 1882, *Life Among the Paiutes*, written by Sarah Winnemucca details the strange legends of red-haired giants who had come to the area by boat, apparently when the area was an inland sea. Twentynine years later the cache of oversized skeletons and artifacts in Lovelock Cave were discovered. As is usually the case, these "legends" were scoffed at by the "authorities" until hard evidence began to show up to support it, and even then nothing was properly investigated.

Whereas the skulls from Lovelock measured no more than 12-14 inches from base to crown, there are others of considerably larger size that have been reported. For instance, the well-known zoologist Ivan T. Sanderson, once received a letter from an engineer that was stationed on the island of Shemya in the isolated Aleutian chain in northwest Alaska during World War II. While bulldozing a group of hills for a future airstrip, the workmen found several sedimentary layers, under which were found the skeletal remains of what appeared to be extremely large humans. Most of the giant skulls measured about 22 to 24 inches from base to crown; whereas, a normal human skull only measures eight inches. Apparently, Sanderson later received an additional letter from another person in the unit, who confirmed the story. Both letters indicated that the Smithsonian Institution had taken possession of the remains, and of course, they were never heard about again.

UNUSUAL TEETH AND BONE STRUCTURES

At this point, the credulity of the reader may become tested, for it gets a bit boring telling story after story of gigantic skeletons and skulls two or three times normal size, regardless of how interesting the details may be. But a few more are in order, and then we'll move on. The central California coastal area near Lompoc is best known for its famous flower fields, but in the field of cryptozoology the region is known for an unusual report[4] of 12-foot human remains that were found while soldiers were digging a storage pit for gunpowder in 1833. After hacking through cemented gravel, a giant skeleton was found surrounded by stone axes, carved shells, and the most unusual porphyry blocks carved with indecipherable symbols. The teeth arrangement of the skull was unlike any that are known of, in that there were double sets of both the upper and lower rows of teeth, or double dentition, as it is called. In the end, the artifacts were reburied in a secret location because superstitious natives felt the discovery was a bad omen. To date, its location has not been rediscovered.

Naturally, if this were the only reported giant with unusual features and dentition in the area it might be considered a fluke or anomalous report. In another account,[5] from nearby Santa Rosa Island, about 55 miles southwest of Santa Barbara, the skeletal remains of a giant man, with double rows of teeth, was also unearthed. Research has suggested that his people may have subsisted on a species of small elephants that once lived on that island. The elephants, and the giants that feasted on them, have long since disappeared, as have any skulls or bones and thus the solid evidence to make sense of this report.

And then there's the teeth themselves. For example there was a discovery made in 1926 from a town outside of Billings, Montana that was reported[6] of an unusually large human-like tooth that had been found in coal deposits deep within the Bearcreek Mutual Coal Mine. The discovery was made by archaeologist J. F. C. Siegfriedt in lumps of coal that had been set aside for inspection. The tooth was said to be about three times normal size and the roots had

---

[4]Stranger than Science, Frank Edwards, Ace Books, NY, 1959, p. 96. Also Jim Brandon, Weird America, E.P. Dutton, NY, 1978, p. 26.

[5]Stranger than Science, Frank Edwards, Ace Books, NY, 1959, p. 97.

[6]The Casper Star-Tribune, July 22nd and 24th, 1979. Also Carbon Country (Montana) News, 11 Nov 1926, p. 5. Also The Casper Tribune Herald, October 22, 1932. Also Frank Edwards, Stranger than Science, Ace Books, NY, 1959, p. 96. Also Jim Brandon, Weird America, E.P. Dutton, NY, 1978, p. 126.

been replaced with iron, and the enamel with carbon. He claims to have carefully preserved both the tooth and the mineral matrix around which it was encased, but the "authorities" were not interested and

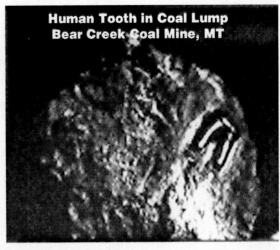

Human Tooth in Coal Lump
Bear Creek Coal Mine, MT

no further mention of it has been seen.

ANOMALOUS SKELETONS

A report from the Big Indian Copper Mine[7] near the Town of LaSal, Utah, in 1973, shows that human-like teeth are not all that have been found while mining for coal. After bulldozing a site in preparation for a mining operation, amateur rock collector Lin Ottinger found a few pieces of brownish teeth and bones. When he found a large bone buried in rock, that was believed to be at least 100 million years old, he stopped digging and returned later with a professor from the University of Utah, Dr. J. P. Marwitt, who proceeded with the excavation. The bones of two human skeletons were unearthed that had not been dismembered or disfigured, indicating they had not been washed into their position nor had they fallen from a higher level. Marwitt then decided that in order to determine an estimated age accurately, the remains would have to be sent back to the laboratory at the University of Utah. Apparently, establishment science lost interest in the bones, and that was the last that was heard of this

[7] F. A. Barnes, "The Case of the Bones in Stone," *Desert Magazine*, February 1975, pp. 36-39. Also Jim Brandon, Weird America, E.P. Dutton, NY, 1978, p. 221.

incredible find. For those unfamiliar with Michael Cremo's several books on forbidden archaeology (see Cremo in the bibliography) which detail the evidence of mankind's prehistoric origins, they are all recommended reading.

From the West Coast to the Midwest, the reports[8] continue near Chatfield and Clearwater, Minnesota, where local mounds that were excavated during the late 1800s were found to contain the skeletal remains of a number of large skeletons. Some were reported as being buried head down, and the skulls had a complete double set of dentition and a recessed forehead, similar to those found at Lompoc Rancho, California and Santa Rosa Island, California.

And on the East Coast, near Moundsville, West Virginia, a number of fort-like foundations can be found, including an octagon-shaped encirclement and other guard-post type "wells" in the hills along the river. Unfortunately, these are severely eroded, but the principal construction can still be found in the form of a large burial mound. In 1838, when Grave Creek Mound was originally

Grave Creek, West Virgina • 200 C.E.

Dunleith, Illinois

Fish Mound, Iowa

[8]St. Paul *Pioneer*, 23 May 1883; 29 Jun 1888. Also St. Paul *Globe*, 12 Aug 1895. Also Jim Brandon, *Weird America*, E.P. Dutton, NY, 1978, pp 117-118.

excavated, it was discovered to contain passages similar to those in the Great Pyramid of Egypt. This earthen pyramid has a network of timber-supported tunnels leading to what appears to be a storage chamber at the middle, and to a burial tomb about seven feet below the surface of the ground. The skeletal remains of what appeared to be a man and woman were found in this lower chamber. Their teeth exhibited an unusual feature, in that the peaks of their molars were conically pointed in shape, as opposed to modern man's, which are squared. Another grave was unearthed above the lower chamber, but below the upper one, which contained another skeleton in a very deteriorated state. There was also a small stone table with 22 runic-like hieroglyphics that was found while excavating near the mound. Luckily, plenty of drawings and casts were made of the object before it disappeared. Since then, "professional" archaeologists have declared it a fake.

Grave Creek Mound, West Virginia • 1847

One last entry, out of many more of anomalous skeletons and skulls, is an account[9] from the 1880s, of a group of distinguished antiquarians that excavated a burial mound near Tioga Point, Pennsylvania. Among those present were Professor W. K. Morehead of Phillips Andover Academy, Professor A. B. Skinner of the American Investigating Museum, and Dr. G. P. Donehoo, a Pennsylvania State historian and distinguished Presbyterian minister. During the dig they unearthed the remains of 68 males with an average height of seven feet. Some of the skulls had bony projections, two inches above the forehead, that appeared to be horn-like buds. Not surprisingly, some of these valuable artifacts were sent to the American Investigating Museum in Philadelphia, but, as usual, they have since disappeared and no one there knows anything about them.

An important point that needs to be made is how few people realize that when the first Spanish explorers made contact in the New World a fair number of the tribes they encountered were of giant stature. Members of some of these tribes were on average 7 or 8 feet tall, with certain individuals being nearly 10 feet tall and possessing the greatest of strength. A number of the large

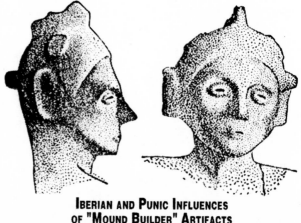

IBERIAN AND PUNIC INFLUENCES OF "MOUND BUILDER" ARTIFACTS

[9]Robert R. Lyman, Forbidden Land as cited in "Giant Skeletons," *Pursuit*, vol. 6 no. 3, July 1973, pp 69-70. Also Jim Brandon, Weird America, E.P. Dutton, NY, 1978, pp 191-192.

skeletal remains that have been found, especially in some of the older and enigmatic mounds that dot the Midwestern and Southern landscapes, may indeed fall into the category of "native" burials and can very well be explained by conventional theories. On the other hand, some of the more bizarre claims, especially when observed as a whole, give the indication there may have been another species, similar to humans yet of a different physiology, that once inhabited North America.

A RACE OF DWARFS

Another curiosity found amongst the mysteries of bizarre human-like remains are reports of miniature adult humanoid mummies. In one such instance,[10] in October of 1932, two men were prospecting for gold in the Pedro Mountains of Wyoming when they found the mummified remains of what appeared to be a mature adult male. The miners were blasting near a stone-walled gulch, and when the dust settled they found the opening of a small cave about four-feet by four-

Chicago Field Museum of Natural History

San Pedro Mummy X-ray
Oct 1932 • Pedro Mtns, WY

[10]Stranger than Science, Frank Edwards, Ace Books, NY, 1959, pp. 118-120.

Chicago Field Museum of Natural History

San Pedro Mummy
Oct 1932 • Pedro Mtns, WY

feet and close to fifteen-feet deep. Inside they found the 14-inch tall San Pedro mummy, as it is now called, weighing about 12 ounces, with its arms and legs crossed, leaning perpendicularly upon a small ledge. According to the authorities, it did not appear to be the body of an infant because of the well-developed and proportional head, which would have been proportionally larger if it had been an infant. It had a broad, thin-lipped mouth, the nose was short and broad, the forehead was flattened, and the skin was a deeply-wrinkled dark brown.

In an unusual display of confidence, the Harvard University Anthropological Department at one time attested for the authenticity of the mummy; the American Museum of Natural History's Dr. Henry Shapiro confirmed that the mummy was of an unknown human type and of enormous age. The Egyptian Department at the

Boston Museum indicated that it corresponds to the look of an Egyptian mummy that had been left unwrapped. At one time the Goodman Family owned this meaningful relic from our past, but they have since moved from the area. Another report claims that the artifact had been donated to the Smithsonian Institution, which, of course, has no record of it. However, the Chicago Field Museum of Natural History does have pictures of the unusual mummy.

Another mysterious mummy was discovered deep inside of Mammoth Cave in Kentucky. The cave is one of the largest natural enclosures of its kind in the world. There has been a number of well preserved cadavers, or "Mammoth Cave mummies" as they are usually called, found here since the cave was first discovered in 1809. One of these mummies, found on a deep ledge of the cavern in 1920, was only three feet tall and had red hair. Another Mammoth Cave mummy has been on occasional display at the State Museum of Anthropology in Lexington.

It has come to my attention that in addition to the unusually small mummies noted above, there have been a number of cases where "shrunken skeletons" have been made through the use of known mummification and embalming processes, resulting in the two small fellows pictured here.

Little Men
Circa 1920

Notice the very human-like proportions and physiology which are unlike that of the San Pedro mummy.

ANCIENT MINING ACTIVITY

And then there's the enigma of prehistoric mining. There are approximately 5,000 prehistoric pit mines[11] of unknown age and origin found in northern Michigan that extend for about 100 miles along the south shore of Lake Superior. Also known as the Arcadian Copper Mines, this is one of the only places on Earth where copper can be found in large quantities in its raw form, as chunks and nuggets. A massive amount, anywhere from 100 million to 500 million pounds, of pure copper appears to have been extracted from these sites. There are still several copper mines functioning in the area and every one of them is located on a site that had been mined in the prehistoric past. However, there has been almost no evidence of any human habitation or settlements, nor any animal bones or human burials anywhere in the area. And yet, the technical engineering that was employed in the construction of some of the mines indicates a highly specialized and organized civilization. In addition, there have been some unusual idol-like artifacts that have been found in the region; some of these can still be found at a private museum in Marble, North Carolina.

Native Americans had no interest in the mines, besides, few aborigine tribes had much use for copper. There are several so-called "Indian" burial mounds, notably in Fall River, MA and Walkerton, IN, that when excavated in the 19th century yielded skeletal remains (up to 9 feet tall)

[11]"Where Did All the Copper Go?" *INFO Journal*, No. 7 (Fall-Winter 1970), pp. 26-28. Also Charles Fort, The Complete Books of Charles Fort, Dover, NY, 1976, p. 147-148. Also Jim Brandon, Weird America, E.P. Dutton, NY, 1978, pp 112-113.

which wore copper artifacts, including copper and/or bronze armor. Dr. Eiler, an archaeologist from Carleton College in Minnesota, has hypothesized that Near-Eastern explorers might have been in the area to mine metals. While commenting on the Indian theory as to the origins of the copper workings Charles Fort wrote: "I think that we've had visitors [and] that they have come here for copper, for instance."

Evidence of mining activity and underground tunnel systems in prehistoric North America are not uncommon. Take for example a report[12] that, in 1954, a pair of existing tunnels were discovered while working a mine owned by the Lion Coal Corporation near Wattis, Utah. At an approximate depth of 8,500 feet, miners found pockets of coal that had been heavily oxidized. Further digging revealed the tunnels, 200 feet apart, that were partially filled with crumpled rock and coal, but that had been mined from both sides. No record of any other mining activity in the area has been recorded and no entrances have ever been found. Due to the nature of mining activity there is no doubt that the location of the tunnels has been lost to history.

UNDERGROUND CAVERNS AND TUNNEL SYSTEMS

Besides evidence of ancient mining, there are also a number of underground chambers and tunnels which have been found over the years. For example, in 1962, Consolidated Edison had planned on building a large electric plant at the north end of where East River Park now stands in New York. When a preliminary soil test was conducted with a large core drilling, at the 200-foot level, the

---

[12]"Another Strange Mine," *Info Journal*, no. 11, September 1973, p. 25. Also Jim Brandon, Weird America, E.P. Dutton, NY, 1978, p. 222.

drill reportedly punched through to a large underground cavern of unascertainable size. As the story goes, the hole was secretly filled in and Consolidated Edison built a nice park over it.

Ten years later, in September 1972, a spokesman for the J.F. Barrett Company of Devon reported finding an unusual tunnel while excavating in Milford, Connecticut for a new sewer. The tunnel appeared to be made partially from dry stone masonry and was more than 200 feet long. At one point there was a masonry arch approximately ten feet across and ten feet high. Naturally, the workmen were there to install a sewer, finished the job as expected, and that's the last anyone's heard about it.

There is also a series of subterranean tunnel systems that have been made from arched masonry structures, found beneath Memphis, Tennessee. The establishment claims that they were built by the military during the civil war. The tunnels that are accessible show a high degree of skill and workmanship, and a great expense of time went into building them, not likely in time of war. There is an entrance to one of them at the east end of Harahan Bridge on I-55. The entrance is between Indiana and Delaware Streets, to the right heading east on Crump Boulevard. It is said to lead to a bigger tunnel that runs lateral to the Mississippi River north along South Third Street towards the center of the city.

And in Lexington, Kentucky, there was a report by G. W. Ranck in the *1872 History of Lexington* describing a gallery of tunnels somewhere beneath this city. The report detailed how, in 1776, hunters from the frontier town of Booneborough found rocks of "peculiar workmanship," behind which was found a tunnel. The small opening inclined sharply into the rock and enlarged to a grand gallery about four feet wide and seven feet high. After a few hundred feet the gallery led to an even larger chamber that was 18 feet high, 100 feet wide and 300 feet in length. Inside of this chamber were found an altar, idols, and about 2,000 human mummies.

SMALLER TUNNELS

Apparently unusual tunnels come in all sizes. In the summer of 1973, in Croften, Maryland, during excavation for a parking lot, workmen found a collection of tunnels which were about 20 inches in diameter. An amateur archaeologist, William Doepkins, concluded that they may have been made by a large rodent, from the claw and tooth marks that were found on the walls. Naturally, the habitat of those oversized rodents was only superficially explored, the lot was leveled, and a parking lot was built over this unusual find.

There is a well-documented case of an unknown tunnel, that originally was discovered in the late 1800s. When searching for a rabbit, a group of hunters discovered an ancient tunnel system made from mortarless dry masonry near the cemetery in Goshen, Massachusetts. The rabbit had jumped into a burrow near the top of a vertical shaft that had been concealed with flagstones covered with sod and shrubbery. The shaft is three and half feet in diameter and about fifteen feet deep, with two horizontal tunnels that branch off, one at the bottom running eastward, and another three feet from the bottom, which travels westward. The tunnels are about two feet wide and about two and a half feet high with flagstone ceilings supported by sidewalls made of stone. The bottom shaft travels about 75 feet, and the upper one about 15 feet, before reaching points where they have collapsed.

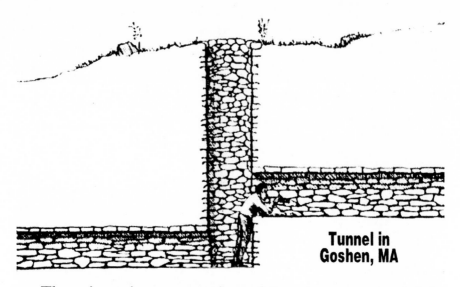

Tunnel in Goshen, MA

There have been a number of theories as to its origin and purpose. One theory is that settlers built it as a shelter from Indian attacks, though none are known to have occurred in the area. Another is that is was part of the "underground railroad," though it was hardly practical for that use. Or that is was a water well, but then why the horizontal shafts, which according to engineers required an enormous amount of effort to bore such narrow shafts, especially in such dense hardpan, at such an unusual right angle, and in such a confined workspace. The structure has more recently been known as "Counterfeiter's Den," from the story that counterfeiters were once caught several miles southwest of the site.

UNDERGROUND CITIES

There is a Piute, or Paiute, Indian legend of an underground city below Death Valley, that they refer to as Shin-Au-av. An Indian guide in the 1920s, Tom Wilson, claimed that his grandfather had discovered catacombs below the ground in the area. He says that they led to an underground city where people spoke an unknown language and wore leather-like clothing. Also in the Death Valley area, a prospector by the name of White says that he had fallen from an abandoned mine near Wingate Pass into a mysterious tunnel. He claims he followed the tunnel which led to a succession of rooms in which he found stacks of gold bricks guarded by hundreds of humanoid mummies that were clad in leather. It is interesting to note that when times were tough Walter Scotty, of nearby Scotty's Castle fame, would wander in the desert for a few days at a time and bring back processed gold that he said he had prospected.

Around the turn of the century, near the city of Chehalis, Washington, there was a man named H F. Forest that claimed he had been prospecting when he came upon a large flat rock "which had been hewn from human hands." He removed the rock and found a cave entrance on the south side of Mount Rainier. He entered the cave and discovered an enclosure about 12-feet high and 60-feet wide, on whose smoothly polished walls could be found "hieroglyphics and figures made by human hands." He explored to a depth of about five miles, occasionally encountering side passages containing ice caves, sulfur springs, hot springs, and cold springs. At one location he came upon human-size bathtubs which had been carved into the bedrock with converging streams of water entering them. Forrest then reportedly came upon an immense underground lake, where a large canoe was chained with silver links to the wall. He removed the canoe and explored the enormous lake for more than a mile in each direction, without reaching shore. Later he came upon a side passage with heavy vaults, one of whose lids was ajar. Inside he found the bodies of two people, a man and a woman,

EXPLORATIONS IN GRAND CANYON

Mysteries of Immense Rich Cavern Being Brought to Light.

JORDAN IS ENTHUSED

Remarkable Finds Indicate Ancient People Migrated From Orient.

The latest news of the progress of the explorations of what is now regarded by scientists as not only the oldest archaeological discovery in the United States, but one of the most valuable in the world, which was mentioned some time ago in the Gazette, was brought to the city yesterday by G. E. Kinkaid, the explorer who found the great underground citadel of the Grand Canyon during a trip from Green river, Wyoming, down the Colorado, in a wooden boat, to Yuma, several months ago. According to the story related yesterday to the Gazette by Mr. Kinkaid, the archaeologists of the Smithsonian Institute, which is financing the explorations, have made discoveries which almost conclusively prove that the race which inhabited this mysterious cavern, hewn in solid rock by human hands, was of oriental origin, possibly from Egypt, tracing back to Ramses. If their theories are borne out by the translation of the tablets engraved with hieroglyphics, the mystery of the prehistoric peoples of North America, their ancient arts, who they were and whence they came, will be solved. Egypt and the Nile, and Arizona and the Colorado will be linked by a historical chain running back to ages which staggers the wildest fancy of the fictionist.

A Thorough Investigation.

Under the direction of Prof. S. A. Jordan, the Smithsonian Institute is now prosecuting the most thorough explorations, which will be continued until the last link in the chain is forged. Nearly a mile underground, about 1480 feet below the surface, the long main

feet ventilation of the cavern, the steady draught that blows through, indicates that it has another outlet to the surface.

Mr. Kinkald's Report.

Mr. Kinkald was the first white child born in Idaho and has been an explorer and hunter all his life, thirty years having been in the service of the Smithsonian Institute. Even briefly recounted, his history sounds fabulous, almost grotesque.

"First, I would impress that the cavern is nearly inaccessible. The entrance is 1486 feet down the sheer canyon wall. It is located on government land and no visitor will be allowed there under penalty of trespass. The scientists wish to work unmolested, without fear of the archaeological discoveries being disturbed by curio or relic hunters. A trip there would be fruitless, and the visitor would be sent on his way. The story of how I found the cavern has been related, but in a paragraph: I was journeying down the Colorado river in a boat, alone, looking for mineral. Some forty-two miles up the river from the El Tovar Crystal canyon I saw on the east wall, stains in the sedimentary formation about 2000 feet above the river bed. There was no trail to this point, but I finally reached it with great difficulty. Above a shelf which hid it from view from the river, was the mouth of the cave. There are steps leading from this entrance some thirty yards to what was, at the time the cavern was inhabited, the level of the river. When I saw the chisel marks on the wall inside the entrance, I became interested, secured my gun and went in. During that trip I went back several hundred feet along the main passage, till I came to the crypt in which I discovered the mummies. One of these I stood up and photographed by flashlight. I gathered a number of relics, which I carried down the Colorado to Yuma, from whence I shipped them to Washington with details of the discovery. Following this, the explorations were undertaken.

The Passages.

"The main passageway is about 12 feet wide, narrowing to 9 feet toward the farther end. About 57 feet from the entrance, the first side-passages branch off to the right and left, along which, on both sides, are a number of rooms about the size of ordinary living rooms of today, though some are 30 or 40 feet square. These are entered by oval-shaped doors and are ventilated by round air spaces through the walls into the passages. The walls are about 3 feet 6 inches in thickness. The passages are chiseled or hewn as straight as could be laid out by an engineer. The ceilings of many of the rooms converge to a center. The side-passages near the entrance run at a sharp angle from the main hall, but toward the rear they gradually reach a right angle in direction.

The Shrine.

"Over a hundred feet from the entrance is the cross-hall, several hundred feet long, in which was found the idol, or image, of the people's god, sitting cross-legged, with a lotus flower or lily in each hand. The cast of the

EXPLORATIONS IN GRAND CANYON

(Continued from Page One.)

which indicates that some sort of ladder was attached. These granaries are rounded, and the materials of which they are constructed, I think, is a very hard cement. A gray metal is also found in this cavern, which puzzles the scientists, for its identity has not been established. It resembles platinum. Strewn promiscuously over the floor everywhere are what people call 'cats' eyes' or 'tiger eyes,' a yellow stone of no great value. Each one is engraved with a head of the Malay type.

The Hieroglyphics.

"On all the urns, on walls over doorways, and tablets of stone which were found by the image are the mysterious hieroglyphics, the key to which the Smithsonian Institute hopes yet to discover. These writings resemble those on the rocks about this valley. The engraving on the tablets probably has something to do with the religion of the people. Similar hieroglyphics have been found in the peninsula of Yucatan, but these are not the same as those found in the orient. Some believe that these cave dwellers built the old canals in the Salt River valley. Among the pictorial writings, only two animals are found. One is of prehistoric type.

The Crypt.

"The tomb or crypt in which the mummies were found is one of the

contain a deadly gas or chemicals used by the ancients. No sounds are heard, but it smells snakey just the same. The whole underground institution gives one of shaky nerves the creeps. The gloom is like a weight on one's shoulders, and our flashlights and candles only make the darkness blacker. Imagination can revel in conjectures and ungodly day-dreams back through the ages that have elapsed till the mind reels dizzily in space."

An Indian Legend.

In connection with this story, it is notable that among the Hopis the tradition is told that their ancestors once lived in an underworld in the Grand Canyon till dissension arose between the good and the bad, the people of one heart and the people of two hearts. Machetto, who was their chief, counseled them to leave the underworld, but there was no way out. The chief then caused a tree to grow up and pierce the roof of the underworld, and then the people of one heart climbed out. They tarried by Paisisvai (Red river), which is the Colorado, and grew grain and corn. They sent out a message to the Temple of the Sun, asking the blessing of peace, good will and rain for the people of one heart. That messenger never returned, but today at the Hopi village at sundown can be seen the old men of the tribe out on the housetops gazing toward the sun, looking for the messenger. When he returns, their lands and ancient dwelling place will be restored to them. That is the tradition. Among the engravings of animals in the cave is seen the image of a heart over the spot where it is located. The legend was learned by W. E. Rollins, the artist, during a year spent with the Hopi Indians. There are two theories of the origin of the Egyptians. One is that they came from Asia; another that the racial cradle was in the upper Nile region. Heeren, an Egyptologist, believed in the Indian origin of the Egyptians. The discoveries in the Grand Canyon may throw further light on human evolution and prehistoric ages.

reportedly between seven and eight feet in height. Both had been laid out on slabs of ice, and were perfectly preserved in a completely frozen state. Forrest left town on 16 Mar 1901, and was never heard from again.

ARIZONA GAZETTE, FRIDAY EVENING,

MARCH 12, 1909.

G. E. Kincaid Reaches Yuma.

G. E. Kincaid of Lewiston, Idaho, arrived in Yuma after a trip from Green River, Wyoming, down the entire course of the Colorado river. He is the second man to make this journey and came alone in a small skiff, stopping at his pleasure to investigate the surrounding country. He left Green River in October, having a small covered boat with oars, and carrying a fine camera, with which he secured over seven hundred views of the river and canyons which are unsurpassed. Mr. Kincaid says one of the most interesting features of the trip was passing through the sluiceways at Laguna dam. He made this perilous passage with only the loss of an oar. Some interesting archaeological discoveries were unearthed and altogether the trip was of such interest that he will repeat it next winter, in the company of friends.

In another report, reminiscent of a scene from *The Twilight Zone*, a traveler to the Mojave Desert north of Baker, California claims he found a small habitation of about 30 dwellings, arranged as a planned community, that had been partially unburied by the shifting of the sands. The structures were said to have been built of wood with massive handmade room timbers. He also claims that there were heavy wooden tables that had been set for a meal. There are no trees found for miles around, nor is there any record of any mining, or other settlement, in the area.

The grand-daddy of all underground city stories can be read in the accompanying article that appeared in the April 5th, 1909 Phoenix Gazette. It describes an underground city in the Grand Canyon that contained a number of unusual artifacts. My apologies for the poor quality of this reproduction. If you would like to read the transcribed text or see a better quality image please visit the website link to this article found at the end of this book.

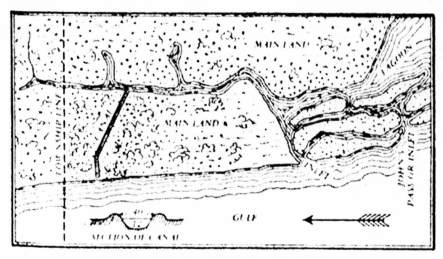

Stone Canals • As Depicted in 1885
Naples, Florida

ANCIENT CANALS

In the 1880s, geologist Andrew Douglass described[13] an ancient canal that ran for a mile and a half between the Naples, Florida, Bay and the Gulf of Mexico. The mysterious canal is "straight as an arrow," about 55 feet across and up to 40 feet deep in places, slicing through both plateaus and sand banks. The bottom of the canal narrows to about twelve feet, and has a two-foot-deep trench about four feet across running down the center. Douglass thought this trench might have been for the keel of a boat. Douglass also wrote "it was a work of enormous labor;" but the question is, what was the purpose, and who in this meagerly populated area could have undertaken it?

Other canals have been found as well, in particular the remains from the Hohokam Indians in the area near present-day Phoenix, Arizona. Their canals were lined with caliche, a type of cement that allowed them to irrigate

---

[13]Andrew E. Douglass, "Ancient Canals on the South-West Coast of Florida," *American Antiquarian*, vol. 7 (1885), pp. 277-285. Also Jim Brandon, Weird America, E.P. Dutton, NY, 1978, p. 60.

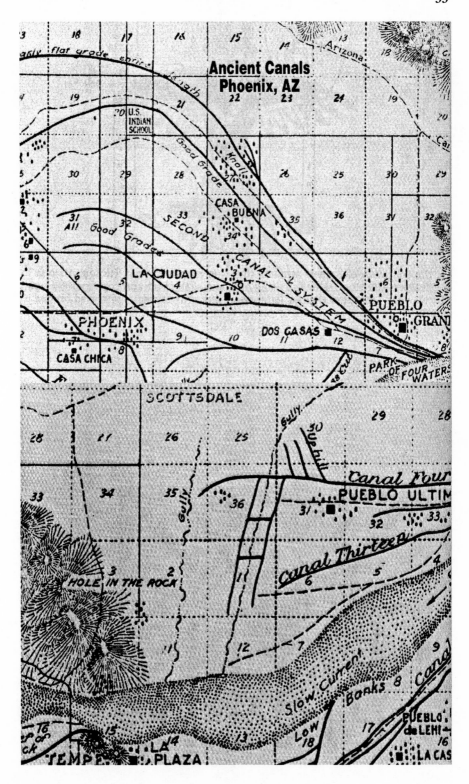

Ancient Canals Phoenix, AZ

much of the Salt and Gila river valleys and create a desert paradise. The Hohokam had built about 250 miles of canals that date from about the year 1300. Some of the old canals can still be seen in various locations, whereas many of the modern canals that crisscross the greater-metropolitan Phoenix area no doubt follow the same routes.

ARTIFACTS UNEARTHED

There have been a number of artifacts which have been brought up from below ground that have baffled the authorities. In August, 1889, an object that has become known as the "Nampa Image" was reportedly[14] pumped up from a well on the property of M. A. Kurtz, a professional well-driller from the Nampa, Idaho area. Kurtz and two workmen claim they were drilling through coarse sand at the 300-foot level when the artifact was brought up by the machinery. The object is obviously humanoid, and is a brownish piece of clay an inch and a half in length. The image had been sent back East for analysis and a professor at Oberlin College, Albert A.

Idaho State Historical Society

**Nampa Image, Idaho
Pumped from Well by
M.A. Kurtz on August 01, 1889**

[14]*Proceedings of the Boston Society of Natural History*, vol. 24, pp 426ff. Also *Scribner's Magazine*, Feb 1890, pp. 235ff. Also Idaho State Historical Society. Also Jim Brandon, Weird America, E.P. Dutton, NY, 1978, pp 73-74.

AN ARCHÆOLOGICAL DISCOVERY IN IDAHO.

By G. Frederick Wright.

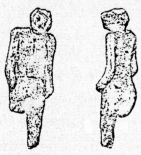

The Nampa Image—actual size.
(Drawn from the object by J. D. Woodward.)

WHILE attention is from time to time being directed to archæological discoveries in the Orient, the public is hardly aware of the rapid accumulation of facts bearing upon the prehistoric condition of America, and revealing an antiquity of the human race on this continent equal to, if not exceeding, that assigned by tangible evidence to man in the Old World. Already rude implements of human manufacture have been discovered at Trenton, N. J., Claymont, Del., Madisonville, O., Medora, Ind., and Little Falls, Minn., in undisturbed gravel deposits dating from the close of the great Ice Age in America. These discoveries correspond, both in the rude character of the implements and in the geological situation, with the palæoliths found in the valley of the Somme, in France, and at various places in southern England. Authorities estimate their age as from seven thousand to one hundred thousand years, according to their interpretation of the date of the close of the glacial epoch.

In Professor J. D. Whitney's report "Upon the Auriferous Gravels of the Sierra Nevada of California," he gives a detailed account of a variety of human remains there discovered, embedded in deposits of equal or even greater age than those just mentioned in Europe and in the Eastern part of the United States. In several instances these remains in California were found in gravel which

had subsequently been covered by deep deposits of lava, and where there had been so much erosion since as to indicate a very great antiquity. Among the most remarkable and best authenticated of these California relics of early man is the celebrated Calaveras skull, reported to have been taken in 1866, by a Mr. Mattison, from the gravel under Table Mountain, near Altaville, Calaveras County, and about one hundred and thirty feet below the surface. Overlying this skull there were four strata of lava and three of gravel, besides the one in which it was found.

Bret Harte has made this skull famous in one of his poems, and I fear has unduly prejudiced the public mind against the real weight of evidence respecting it. This humorous poet, after giving his own confused surmises as to the tale of geologic history which the skull might tell, heard these hollow accents from the skull itself:

> "Which my name is Bowers, and my crust was busted
> Falling down a shaft in Calaveras County,
> But I'd take it kindly if you'd send the pieces
> Home to old Missouri!"

A French critic actually took Harte's poetry for a pure statement of fact.

But, notwithstanding these gibes, there is so strong a chain, both of direct and circumstantial evidence, supporting the genuineness of the Calaveras skull, that there would probably have been little question about it had it not encountered the strong preconceived theories of two important and influential classes of people, namely, the orthodox theologians and the uncompromising evolutionists. The theologians were prejudiced because they thought the skull was made out to be

Rear View of the Image.

Wright, found it was half clay and half quartz, and that the fractured right leg was not recent. Then, Dr. G. Frederick Wright (no relation), of the Boston Society of Natural History went to Nampa to investigate the circumstances in which it was discovered. He inspected the steam-driven pump and drilling machinery. He then questioned Kurtz at length, and reported to the Society that "there is no grounds to question the fact that this image came up in the sand pump from the depth reported." Professor F. W. Putnam, also of Boston, stated "the cementing of quartz grains by iron molecules under the image's right arm was evidence of great age." The Idaho State Historical Society, in Boise, has retained caretakership of the artifact, one of only a few surviving objects of a similar nature that have been found in America.

In another similar report,[15] from August 1870, near Lawnridge, Illinois, there was an artifact that was brought up with drilling residues while bor-

Coin Pumped from Well • 1870
Lawnridge, Peoria County, Illinois

ing an artesian well at a depth of 125 feet, according to Jacob W. Moffit of Chillicothe. The coin-like object was about the size of a quarter-dollar of the era. The illustration shows a man-like being riding some sort of bird. Scientist William E. DuBois examined the coin carefully and stated that the coin showed no signs of hammering and the patterns on it appeared to have been etched with chemicals, rather than being stamped or engraved. DuBois also felt

[15]William E. DuBois, "On a Quasi Coin Reported Found in a Boring in Illinois," *Proceedings of the American Philosophical Society*, vol. 12, no. 86, 01 Dec 1871, pp. 224-228. Also Jim Brandon, Weird America, E.P. Dutton, NY, 1978, p. 82.

that the coin must have been passed through a rolling mill and that there were other signs of work in a machine shop. He concluded by stating "how it got into such a deep place, supposing it to be a bona fide discovery, which I cannot call into question, is a very perplexing point . . ."

And this most unusual report,[16] from 1851, of an unusual object unearthed in Dorchester, Massachusetts while blasting to expand a house of worship operated by the Reverend Mr. Hall. Amongst the tons of debris scattered about, workmen discovered a "metallic vessel in two parts." The object was approximately four inches wide by six inches high, was bell-shaped, and showed a high degree of craftsmanship. Apparently, it had been blown out of solid pudding stone from 15 feet below the surface. The *Scientific American* stated that it was satisfied that it had occurred as reported.

Scientific American • 1851

A Relic of a By-Gone Age.

A few days ago a powerful blast was made in the rock at Meeting House Hill, in Dorchester, a few rods south of Rev. Mr. Hall's meeting house. The blast threw out an immense mass of rock, some of the pieces weighing several tons and scattered small fragments in all directions. Among them was picked up a metallic vessel in two parts, rent asunder by the explosion. On putting the two parts together it formed a bell-shaped vessel, 4½ inches high, 6½ inches at the base 2½ inches at the top, and about an eighth of an inch in thickness. The body of this vessel resembles zinc in color, or a composition metal, in which there is a considerable portion of silver. On the sides there are six figures of a flower, or bouquet, beautifully inlaid with pure silver, and around the lower part of the vessel a vine, or wreath, inlaid also with silver. The chasing, carving, and inlaying are exquisitely done by the art of some cunning workman. This curious and unknown vessel was blown out of the solid pudding stone, fifteen feet below the surface. It is now in the possession of Mr. John Kettell. Dr. J. V. C. Smith, who has recently travelled in the East, and examined hundreds of curious domestic utensils, and has drawings of them, has never seen

---

[16]*Scientific American*, 1851. Also Charles Fort, The Complete Books of Charles Fort, Dover, NY, 1976, p. 130. Also Jim Brandon, Weird America, E.P. Dutton, NY, 1978, p. 103.

It was believed to be an alloy of silver and zinc and had six figures of a bouquet around the circumference and a wreath-like decoration around the base, both of which had been beautifully inlaid with silver.

THE COGSTONES OF THE TOPANGA CULTURE

Artifacts of significant archaeological interest have been found[17] throughout the Los Angeles basin, the western half of San Diego county, and on certain isles in the Channel Islands chain not far from shore. The most famous relics from this lost civilization are known as the "cog stones of the Topanga Culture" and have been found mostly in the Bolsa Chica State Beach area. These California cog stones, as they are commonly called, are gear-like stones ranging in size from two to six inches in diameter, with a thickness up to two inches. The cog stones come with different characteristics such as cups, cusps, hemispherical grooves and dents, sprocketed teeth around the edges, as well as cookie-cutter patterns. Most all of these features occur at precise and repeating intervals, and about 15 percent had a single hole bored through the center. Many times these holes are narrower on one side, have elliptical sides, are conical, or double conical, where the entry point holes are narrower on either side than at the midpoint.

One of the artifacts in particular has a striking anomaly in that it has perfectly square perforation in the middle, something that would be troublesome to duplicate even with our present machine shop technology. Many of the

---

[17]Hal Eberhart, "The Cogged Stones of Southern California," *American Antiquity*, vol. 26, no. 3, (1961), pp. 361-370. Also Jim Brandon, Weird America, E.P. Dutton, NY, 1978, pp. 28-29.

cog stones are found at the circa 6,000 B.C.E. strata, containing artifacts that are some of the most primitive found in North America. The uniqueness of these artifacts are not so much their being found primarily at the estimated 8,000 year old level, but in the fact that a cog-stone-only level occurs below this one that is of a correspondingly older age. It seems pretty obvious that the later peoples may have found the relics of the previous culture and they thus became deposited in their strata. Questions remain on the origins of this earlier tribe.

ROMAN RELICS OF ARIZONA

More unusual artifacts were unearthed[18] in 1924, when Charles E. Manier found a riveted lead cross and other artifacts of a mysterious nature near Tucson, Arizona. The cross had been protruding from where the roadway had cut through an embankment on a bluff on the west side of the Santa Cruz River. Nearly three dozen artifacts were eventually found at this site. One of the first crosses to

"Roman Relics"
Tucson, Arizona

be unearthed was bound together by rivets; and when each half was separated they revealed Latin and Hebrew inscriptions, but of an unknown style and form.

---

[18]Arizona Historical Society. Also Jim Brandon, Weird America, E.P. Dutton, NY, 1978, pp 13-14.

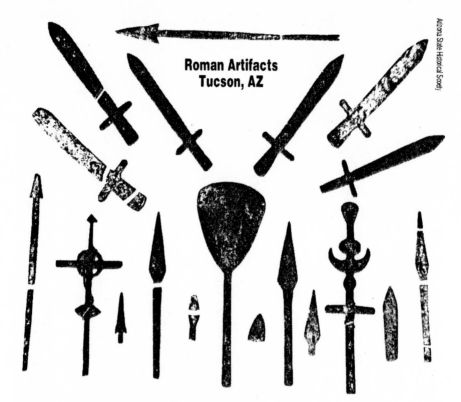

**Roman Artifacts
Tucson, AZ**

Reminiscent of Havisupal Canyon, one of the crosses had, as its only inscription, a depiction of what could only be a dinosaur. A number of the symbols revealed possible mystical origins, including emblems of freemasonry, in particular the Masonic square and compass. Another cross that was found had a snake entwined around it and displayed a number of indecipherable symbols and a few Hebrew letters. Many of the artifacts have an esoteric element associated with them in one way or another.

Manier and his friend Thomas Bent, who owned the property and therefore the artifacts, had brought in skilled professionals with irreproachable credentials to assist in the excavation. The establishment's final verdict was that a catholic boy of Hispanic decent, Vicente Odohui, who had lived in the area; or possibly Mormons trying to support doctrine, had planted the artifacts beforehand. These both may be plausible explanations for the discovery of these objects, except when they are viewed together with other artifacts

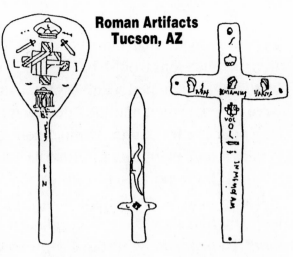

**Roman Artifacts
Tucson, AZ**

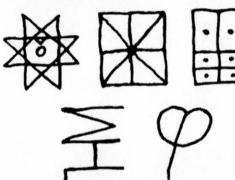

**Greco-Roman Rock Carvings
Clarksville, Virginia**

of a similar nature. Many of the Tucscon artifacts have been donated to the Arizona Historical Society and are on occasional display in Tucson.

Then there's the report[19] from the 1940s of a farmer in Clarksville, Virginia named James V. Howe, who found quite a few swords, weapons, chisels and even threaded nuts. Other artifacts unearthed include a bronze spindle whorl, a broken bronze cup, and other pieces of bronze. According to historian Charles M. Boland, the bronze cup is very similar to Pompeian cups of the Roman Empire. Howe eventually began working sites as far away as Brunswick County, 50 miles to the east. Howe determined that since there were no traces of tin or copper at the sites, the bronze must have been brought in from elsewhere.

---

[19]Charles M. Boland, "They All Discovered America," p. 61. Also Jim Brandon, Weird America, E.P. Dutton, NY, 1978, pp. 227-228

It should come as no surprise that in 1951 an announcement was made that the river would be dammed and the area in question would be flooded, so the Smithsonian Institution conducted a cursory excavation. But the results were inconclusive, and they declined to run carbon dating techniques to try and determine their age. Many other universities and institutions refused Howe's request to date them. At last report, some of the bronze and iron relics can still be found at the Smithsonian, if one knows where to look, though they have been classified as "origin uncertain." Unfortunately, most of Howe's excavation sites are now underwater.

ELEPHANT SLABS OF NEW MEXICO

At the beginning of the twentieth century, there were two small stone tablets found near Flora Vista, New Mexico by a local boy. Inscribed onto the tablets were indecipherable hieroglyphics of an unknown origin. One particularly unusual aspect is that there are two small elephants inscribed on one of the "elephant slabs," as they have come to be called.

Elephant Slabs
Flora Vista, New Mexico

This is unusual indeed, since according to the generally "accepted" belief man could not have possibly inhabited North America when elephants roamed freely, so where did its engraver obtain knowledge of the pachyderms? Paleontologists claim that elephants became extinct in North America nearly 40,000 years ago, long before aborigines had first crossed the Bering Straits.

A clue may be found in the fact that a large number of the symbols were similar to those alphabets used in the Near East in about 1,100 B.C.E. Travelers from the Mediterranean region would have had the knowledge of elephants. There was also a smattering of other characters across the rocks, mostly symbols and characters of unknown meaning. The site that the slabs were reportedly found dates to about the year 1,000 C.E. Another artifact, a jug dated to about the same time, was found near Shiprock Mountain, to the northwest of Flora Vista. An elephant figure was found etched into that one as well. Because the elephant slabs don't fit in with contemporary thinking they have been rejected as fakes by archaeologists. They were last on display at Tucson's Arizona State Museum.

INSCRIPTIONS UNEARTHED

There have been a number of strange and undecipherable inscriptions found in various parts of the United States. While many of these depictions can be attributed to known cultures and/or peoples, there are several notable exceptions whose origin and age cannot be conclusively determined. For example, in the fall of 1868, near Hammondsville, Ohio, workmen at a coal strip mine discovered a large slate wall behind a massive chunk of coal. The wall reportedly was scattered with undecipherable hieroglyphics, in lines about three inches apart. Local experts could not figure out what to make of it, and before more qualified scholars could arrive the wall disintegrated a short time after its exposure to fresh air.

And in Nov 1829, as reported by Professor Silliman in the *American Journal of Science and Arts*, a block of marble was being quarried from a depth of 70 to 80 feet near Philadelphia, Pennsylvania that bore what appeared to be two inscribed letters. As the block was being cut into slabs, a rectangular cavity of about one and a half inches by five-eighths of an inch containing two raised letters was revealed by the saw blade. The letters coincided with our modern-day letters "I" and "U" with the "U" being in angular block form.

Of the many reports of ancient inscriptions, there is one[20] that received a great deal of attention at the time it was first reported, and thus is very well documented, including several renderings. It was discovered in March, 1891, when an unusual stone with bizarre

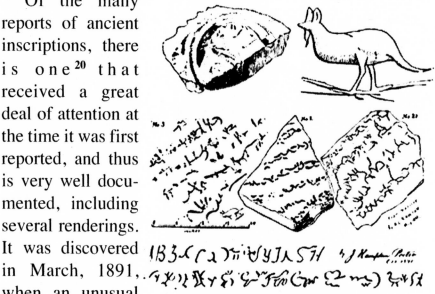

**Rock Wall Carvings • Discovered in 1891
Bradley County, Tennessee**

inscriptions was found by a farmer named J. H. Hooper on a wooded ridge in Bradley County, Tennessee. He thought he had found the headstone to a grave, but as he dug deeper he uncovered other stones that formed a wall of three courses. In all, the wall was about two feet thick, eight feet

[20]A. L. Rawson, "The Ancient Inscription on a Wall at Chatata, Tennessee," *Transactions of the New York Academy of Science*, vol. 11, 09 Nov 1891, pp. 26-28. Also Charles Fort, The Complete Books of Charles Fort, Dover, NY, 1976, p. 158. Also Jim Brandon, Weird America, E.P. Dutton, NY, 1978, pp 204-205.

high, and for about sixteen feet of its length, measured
from the north end, it was covered with nearly 900 symbols and letters, arranged in wavy, nearly parallel and diag-
onal lines. The wall was traced and examined in many
places for a distance of nearly a thousand feet, its course
marked on the surface with stones like that outlined in the
illustration that projected a few inches above the surface at
intervals of twenty-five to thirty feet. A few of the inscriptions, in particular, were of a very unusual nature, one
depicting a bearded kangaroo-like animal with two duck-
like feet. An interesting aspect about the slab itself is the
fact that after the letters had been carved onto the wall, a
dark red cement was applied and then a closely fitting
external course of stones was placed upon the whole, as if
someone had tried to conceal the wall. There were also a
number of what appeared to be oriental characters, which
the authorities claim were "accidental." The origin and
date of these inscriptions remains unknown.

Also in Tennessee, near Sweetwater, in 1885 archaeologists from the Smithsonian Institution found a stone slab

Pisa Rock Carving • Alton, IL

that was covered with undecipherable inscriptions. Not surprisingly, the strange object was catalogued as being Cherokee Indian. A scholar on Mediterranean culture from Brandeis University, Dr. Cyrus Gorden, postulated that the characters on the stone, and another found near Fort Benning, Georgia, looked very similar to the lettering of the Minoan culture that became extinct in about 1,100 B.C.E. Amazingly, the Smithsonian Institution did not "misplace" the object, and in more recent years an archaeologist from the Museum of Art in Columbus, Georgia; a Joseph B. Mahan, revived interest in the object. Whether the Smithsonian Institution still possesses this object, or any of the countless others mentioned in this book, remains to be seen.

STAIRWAY TO NOWHERE

Pisa Rock Drawing in 1854 Alton, IL

There is an 80-foot high sculpted limestone outcropping, known as the Balustrade Bluffs, that runs for about two miles along the Mississippi River to the northwest of Alton, Illinois.[21] Authorities have once again

---

[21]Stephen D. Peet, "A Map of Emblematic Mounds...," *American Antiquarian*, vol. 11 March 1889, pp. 73ff. Also Jim Brandon, Weird America, E.P. Dutton, NY, 1978, p. 79.

declared that this entire area was caused by selectively random erosion. At the center of this huge geo-anomaly is a "Stairway to Nowhere," whose beginning and end are just there, nowhere. It is also known as the Grand Staircase, and if it is a natural formation, it is a strange one indeed.

At the base of the staircase is the Piasa Rock Carving, or rather, the one that has been recently painted on top of it based on a drawing published in 1839, in Germany, by Henry Lewis. His illustrations showed a group of Indian shamans on canoes pointing at a figure with a bearded face and horns; however, drawings by earlier explorers were less dramatic, and have been closer to reality.

FOOTPRINTS IN STONE

There are many reports of mysterious human-like footprints that have been found cast in stone, presumably having been laid down while the ground was still soft. In one

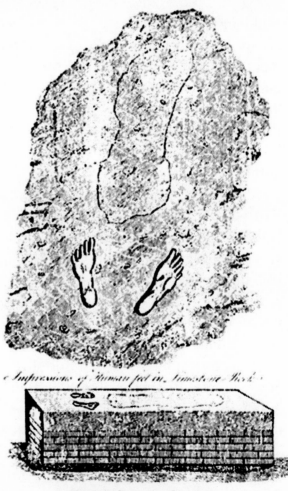

**Footprints in Stone
St. Louis, Missouri • 1820**

such case, from January 1938, a set of ten human-like footprints were reported[22] in Rockcastle County, Kentucky, by geologist Wilbur G. Burroughs. The footprints had been molded into a sandstone rock formation that was found in strata from the Upper Carboniferous Period, ending approximately 310 million years ago. The earliest ancestors of modern man are believed to be about 3.5 million years old. An interesting feature of these unusually large footprints was that they measured about six inches across in width, while only being nine or ten inches in length.

In another unusual find, in the summer of 1882, at a quarry excavation in the yard of the State Prison in Carson City, Nevada, a number of footprints were found[23] in a sandstone layer

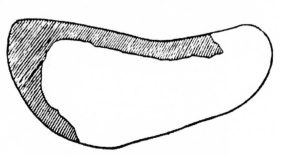

**Footprint Found in Pilocene Stone
Dated to 10 Million Years Old
Carson City, Nevada • 1882**

belonging to the Upper Pliocene, ending about 10 million years ago. Among the prints can be found those which look like birds, elephants, horses, wolves, and six groups that resemble left and right human footprints with a straddle width of about 18 inches. A normal human straddle with is about 5 inches. The prints were about 8 inches wide and 18 to 20 inches in length. Writing in the *American Journal of Science*, scientist O. C. Marsh ruled out them being of human origin due to their size and the width of their stride, instead he was certain they had been made by a "large

[22]*New York Times*, 20 Jan 1938, p. 25. Also Jim Brandon, Weird America, E.P. Dutton, NY, 1978, pp 94-95.

[23]O. C. Marsh, "Footprints in Nevada," *American Journal of Science*, vol. 126 (Jul-Dec 1883), pp. 139-140. Also Jim Brandon, Weird America, E.P. Dutton, NY, 1978, pp 130-131.

sloth" whose "hind feet covered the impressions of those in the front."

In a little place called Brayton, Tennessee, there are also a number of unusual footprints which have been molded into solid rock. They appear to have been made by a giant horse, and nearby are some human-like footprints that are about thirteen inches wide and which show six

**Dinosaur and Human Prints
Glen Rose, TX**

toes. And in another well-known occurrence,[24] there have been numerous enigmatic human-like footprints found embedded in stone in Dinosaur Valley State Park, in Texas. What makes these prints so unusual is not only their enormous size, but the fact that they are found alongside, and in some cases overlapping, obvious dinosaur tracks which are believed to be about 135 million years old. It is interesting to note "establishment science's" reaction to this one: they accept the dinosaur tracks as genuine and dismiss the humanoid ones as fake, made by practical

[24]John Green, "Fossil Tracks at Glen Rose," *Pursuit*, no. 36, Fall 1976, pp. 83-85. Also Jim Brandon, Weird America, E.P. Dutton, NY, 1978, pp 216-217.

jokers, Indians, locals, or whomever. It is obvious that the prints are not fakes because of the ridges that were pushed up around the edges when the foot originally sank

Fossilized Footprints From 300,000 million year old rock Antelope Springs, Utah

into the mud, which then eventually turned to stone. Many of these prints have since been destroyed by a flood that inundated the area in 1978, but a few still remain.

There is another strange case of what may be the oldest fossil footprint found to date, a fossilized human sandal print found near Antelope Springs, Utah, in June of 1968. This incredible discovery, found by William J. Meister, an amateur fossil collector on a rock and fossil hunting expedition with his family, was embedded in Cambrian rock that dates between 300 and 600 million years old. Meister

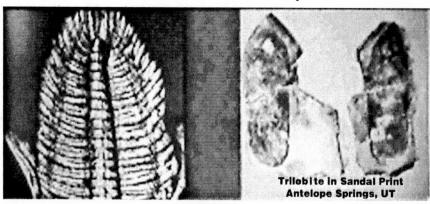

Trilobite in Sandal Print
Antelope Springs, UT

discovered the fossil after splitting open a two inch slab of rock with his hammer, the rock falling open "like a book." On the one side was a layer of trilobites, on the other was the sandaled footprint, with trilobites embedded within. Like a human shoe print, the sandal print was 10 1/2 inches long by 3 1/2 inches wide, and slightly indented at the heel.

An unusual aspect of this find, besides the fact that a supposed late Paleozoic human wore sandals, is the actuality that the trilobites embedded in the footprint suggest that the two were laid down at the same time, when the rock was still mud. Trilobites flourished beginning 600 million years ago and then became extinct 280 million years ago. They were a small marine invertebrate that were related to other crustaceans like shrimp and crab. According to conventional wisdom, modern humans arrived on the scene no earlier than two to three million years ago. Man has been wearing footwear for only the past few thousand years.

Meister took the rock to the University of Utah, where he showed it to Melvin Cook, a professor of metallurgy, who suggested that he show the rock to the experts in the geology department. He was unable to find a geologist to inspect the fossil, so he turned to a local newspaper, the *Deseret News*, and gained national recognition for the find. Other fossilized footprints have been found in the area. The site was examined by a consulting geologist, one Dr. Clifford Burdick, from Tucson, Arizona, in July of 1968, who soon found fossilized imprints of a child's foot. "The impression," he said, "was about six inches in length, with the toes spreading, as if the child had never yet worn shoes, which compress the toes. There does not appear to be much of an arch, and the big toe is not prominent." Dr. Burdick stated: "The rock chanced to fracture along the front of the toes before the fossil print was found. On a cross section, the fabric of the rock stands out in fine laminations, or bedding planes. Where the toes pressed into the soft material, the laminations were bowed downward from the horizontal, indicating a weight that had been pressed into the mud."

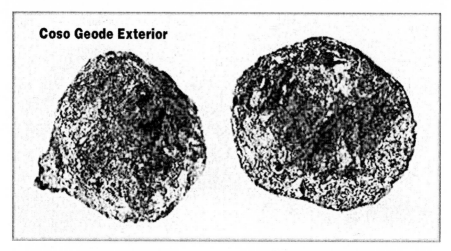

Coso Geode Exterior

THE COSO GEODE

In February 1961, three rock hunters, Wallace Lane, Virginia Maxey and Mike Mikesell found what appeared[25] to be a fossil-encrusted geode near Olancha, California. It reportedly sat around for a while, and when it was finally cut open it severely damaged a new diamond saw blade. Unlike a normal geode, the

Coso Geode X-Ray

exterior was primarily of hardened clay with a mixture of organic matter. Within the crust were also found objects

Coso Geode with Ruler

that appear to be a washer and a nail. In fact, the object was not like a real geode, it was of a different composition, and it did not have a hollow center like most common geodes. Instead there was a nearly perfect cylindrical core of a hard white ceramic that had a 2-mm shiny metal shaft running down the center. In addition, when the core was removed it left a partial hexagonal cavity in the shell of the rock. X-rays of the object show that it has many features of the copper and porcelain spark plugs used in early gasoline engines. However, testing has revealed that some of the fossils in the outer crust may be as much as 500,000 years old. There are a number of what appear to be abandoned mines in the area, though none that are known to have been worked since the white man arrived in the area. Recent analysis of this interesting artifact seems to indicate it may have been a hoax, though it is uncertain how the hoaxers profited from it.

[25]*INFO Journal*, No 4 (Spring 1969). pp 4-13. Also Jim Brandon, Weird America, E.P. Dutton, NY, 1978, pp. 23-24.

OUR CATACLYSMIC PAST

There has been a great deal written on the tumultuous geological history that has occurred here on planet Earth (See Velikovsky, Cremo, Sitchin, and others in the bibliography).

Our Cataclysmic Past?

If there were an advanced civilization that existed on Earth before recorded history began, could it have been, like the famed city-state of Atlantis, been laid asunder by cataclysmic events that have occurred in the remote past? Besides what we've looked at so far, there is some physical evidence in the form of geological anomalies, such as the one[26] at the tip of Point Loma near San Diego, CA, which has many authorities baffled. There are hundreds of metamorphic and lava-formed boulders which become revealed at low tide at this site just to the west of downtown San Diego. There are rocks and boulders on the bluff, 350 feet above the shoreline, the largest of which, weighing about 50 tons, lies about 30 feet from the area lighthouse. The aberration is to explain how all these rocks ended up here, especially the ones topside on the bluff,

[26]Allan O. Kelley, "Erratic Boulders on Point Loma," *Scientists Forum*, vol. 1, part 3, January 1971, Escondido, CA, pp. 80-81. Also Jim Brandon, Weird America, E.P. Dutton, NY, 1978, p. 35.

since the closest source for the rock is about 18 miles to the southwest on north Coronado Island. One of the plausible explanations is that, at a time in the not too distant past, there had been widespread and catastrophic ocean flooding which uplifted the rocks to their present location. There are sites where similar deposits have been found throughout San Diego County, in particular a 30-acre site near Alpine that is about 20 miles east of San Diego at an elevation of 1,500 feet.

Also of interest is the Willcockson fossil beds, found in Marble Falls, Arkansas, which contain the fossilized remains of tropical palm trees, saber-tooth tigers, American rhinoceroses, and other tropical flora and fauna that theoretically shouldn't be found this far north. There is also a massive marine fossil bed near Lake Okeechobee, Florida that dates from the Pleistocene era. The 40-foot layer of deposits contains mostly mollusks and other marine life that are now found only in remote parts of the Pacific Ocean. In addition, the upper layers of the fossil pit contain a number of disjointed bones of what are believed to be large terrestrial animals, presumably mammals. Well-known archaeologist Dr. J. Manson Valentine thought that the fossil pit was a sea bed, and that the layers had been laid down as long as 30,000 years ago. Valentine believed this was additional evidence that a world-wide catastrophic flood had occurred in recent history. He also suggested that the fossil deposits that only occur in the Pacific could have been laid down by cataclysmic waves before there was a substantial land bridge in Central America.

Another cataclysmic anomaly, this time out in the Pacific Ocean, sits on top of the extinct Mauna Kea volcano, in Hawaii, where there appear to be remnants of clear glacial ice. According to Dr. Alfred Woodcock,[27] the ice conceivably dates back to the Pleistocene Era, and therefore may be as ancient as 10,000 to 25,000 years old. The question which must be asked is why tropical insects can be found within the ice in these frigid conditions, and how and when a glacier of considerable size formed in the middle of one of the world's warmest tropical oceans.

THEY ALL DISCOVERED AMERICA

From here on, we're going to be going over some of the more mundane entries. While still interesting in their own respect, most are no doubt the result of more recent human activity and habitation. For those not familiar with the notion of pre-Columbian

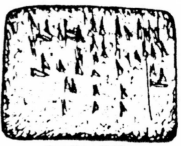

**Cuneiform Writing
Hearn Tablet, Georgia
Dated to 1000-2000 B.C.E.**

explorations to North America, suffice it to say that "everyone discovered America" including evidence of explorations by the Assyrians, Babylonians, Celts, Chinese, Egyptians, Greeks, Hindus, Minoans, Nordics, Pacific Islanders, Phoenicians, Romans, Vikings, the

**Cuneiform Table • Dated 2042 B.C.E.
Found in Chief Joseph's Medicine
Pouch in 1877 • Wyoming**

Welsh, and West Africans, just to name a few. Artifacts and remnants of these once-great civilizations, like the cuneiform tablets pictured here, have been found throughout North America. Some of the following entries are no doubt a result of these worldwide excursions.

---

[27]Quoted by *INFO Journal*, no. 7 (Fall/Winter 1970), p. 48. Also Jim Brandon, *Weird America*, E.P. Dutton, NY, 1978, p. 70.

UNDERWATER STRUCTURES

There are some underwater structures in Tarpon Springs, Florida that are similar to those found near Bimini and Andros in the Caribbean. Well-known archaeologist Dr. J. Manson Valentine describes the artifacts as "obviously cut stone disks" that are possible sun symbols used in archaic ceremonies. There are also a number of 8-inch diameter hexagonal stones of unknown origin or purpose found in the area. They might have been used for some type of cobble-stone road or boundary lines, that, even still, run onto the shore from a level platform standing in about four feet of water offshore.

Valentine believed that the structures may eventually be associated with the enigmatic Arawak people who are believed to have built a similar complex of square courts cut into the bedrock on the West Indian island of St. Lucia. Although the Arawak were said to have had colonies in the Gulf states, Florida, the Bahamas, and the Caribbean, they were believed to have been headquartered in northern South America. Valentine believed that the Arawaks were in fact a blond race of bearded tribesmen related to the Inca and early Polynesians.

ENIGMATIC STRUCTURES

Just north of the 33rd parallel, along the Gila River, lies Cochran Ghost Town,[28] a place of mystery and intrigue if there ever was one. There is a row of five domed structures along this prominent river in Arizona that are as beautiful as they are baffling. The Beehives, as they have become known, stand 32 feet tall and are made from stone granite blocks held in place without mortar, in a feat of masonic

---

[28]Ronald L. Ives, "The Cochran Coke Ovens," *Journal of Arizona History*, Summer 1972, pp 73-81.

engineering. There is a three-foot by six-foot door at the front and a three-foot by five-foot opening at the upper rear of each one.

Unfortunately, there are no documented sources concerning the origin of the domes at this site. Some people claim they were built by an ancient Indian tribe from Central America, since strikingly similar beehive-like structures have been found there. Others believe early Spaniards were responsible for building them. One theory of particular interest is that they were built as lead smelters by Phoenicians who arrived here circa 1500 B.C.E. and founded a city nearby, which later became Phoenix. A professor from Northern Arizona University, Dr. Ronald Ives, writes of the Phoenician theory that "a considerable amount of evidence suggests either one or more pre-Columbian visits to the area by Europeans . . ." In fact, as can be seen in subsequent books in this series, there is an accumulating mound of evidence supporting pre-Columbian visits by not only European explorers, but those from the Far East, the Middle East, and the Near East as well.

Another mystery can be found out in the Pacific Ocean where there is an enigmatic shrine of unknown origin on the uninhabited 200 yard by 1,300 yard Necker Island about 300 miles northwest of the Island of Kauai, Hawaii. There are a number of paved terraces of considerable size, each with a row of monoliths on raised platforms on one end. Nearby, there are other slabs standing upright amongst other related stone artifacts. In fact, a number of small artifacts have been found at this site, including idols carved from stone that are unlike other Polynesian artifacts found in the Hawaiian Islands.

MYSTERY WALLS

In the hills above Oakland and Berkeley in California there are some ancient walls of mysterious origin. Some of the most startling examples are in the Botanical Garden section of the Tilden Regional Park northeast of the University of California at Berkeley campus. It is estimated that the walls extend about 7 miles, amongst the steep cliff and dense undergrowth, of the San Pablo Ridge. They are mainly found around the Grizzly and Vollmer peaks, overlooking Redwood Canyon, and on the south slope of Mt. Baldy. The height of the walls averages about 3 feet and the width about 4 feet in most places. They have been made from loose piles of rocks arranged in curved, intersecting, but mostly straight lines. Some of the rocks weigh upwards of a ton, though most are only a few hundred pounds. The authorities claim these structures were used as Indian livestock corrals or game traps, even though they would have been ineffective for either purpose.

Eight miles to the southwest of Berryville, Arkansas, a rocky outcrop contains a uniformly rectangular doorway[29] about four feet high and 1 1/2 feet wide that leads through a winding passage to a small circular enclosure. It has been labeled a treasure chamber or a "Spanish mine" but its extremely low ceiling height would invalidate either of those claims. This site is on private land between Brushy creek and the Prescott farm.

UNUSUAL STONE STRUCTURES

There are a large number of anomalous stone structures that can be found throughout southern Colorado and northern New Mexico. There are at least a half-dozen known

[29]Arkansas traveler and folklorist Tom Townsend. Also Jim Brandon, Weird America, E.P. Dutton, NY, 1978, p. 15.

sites[30] in Apishapa River Canyon in Colorado. Many of them are associated with petroglyphs that have been found in canyons and valleys near each site. The structures in this area are always found in pairs: a simpler one to the west or northwest, and a more elaborate site across the

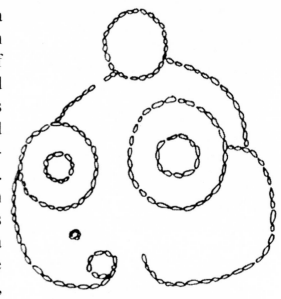

**Stone Circles and Enclosures
Apishapa Canyon, Colorado**

Apishapa River and usually at a lower elevation. They are normally situated on cliffs, bluffs, plateaus, or mesas, within a line of site with each other, and with landmarks in the surrounding landscape.

All of the sites consist mostly of ellipsoidal lines and circles that have been made from sandstone slabs. The slabs themselves are usually about eight to ten inches thick, sometimes sit as high as a yard off the ground, and exhibit a moderate to extreme amount of weathering. The first pair is near the mouth of Apishapa Canyon, looking over the prairie to the north. The more intricate of the pair consists of several circles, the largest about twenty feet in diameter, with a concentric circle within it. There is a stone wall surrounding the site with a doorway on the west side.

---

[30]E. B. Renaud, "Indian Enclosures of Colorado and New Mexico," Unpublished monograph of the Department of Anthropology, University of Denver, 1942), pp. 13-20. Also Robert K. G. Temple, The Sirius Mystery, (London: Sedgwick and Jackson, 1976), pp 147-149. Also Jim Brandon, Weird America, E.P. Dutton, NY, 1978, pp 47-48.

Across the river, which is far below, is the other half of the pair. It includes only two non-contiguous circles that run parallel to the river.

The next pair of sites can be found about a mile further upstream, and the third pair is about five miles to the southwest from the first site. It is at a place where the Apishapa Canyon is intersected by South Canyon from the west. This site is unusual in that it uses much larger stones than any of the others in the area. It incorporates three groups of six circular structures that have been placed side-by-side. Each of the circular structures has a stone pillar, implicative of phallic standing stones found elsewhere; four of these can still be found standing. At the eastern end of the site is an underground passageway that was made by covering over cloven spaces in the rock.

In West Virginia there are a number of wall-like structures that run north and south for about three miles on a lofty summit in a barren environment. The Mount Carbon Stone Walls, as they are known, are similar in their slab-like construction to those found near

**Unusual Stone Walls
Mt. Carbon, West Virginia**

Apishapa River Canyon, Colorado, though not as complex or consistent in form. There are several mounds, even one shaped like a turtle, in the center of the complex made from both earth and rock fabrication. There are also some flint quartz rocks of considerable size incorporated into the structure that must have been brought up this 2,300-foot peak, since none occurs naturally at this level. In addition, evidence of worked flint instruments has been found near the mounds.

CAHOKIA MOUND COMPLEX

The Cahokia Mounds complex is a 224-acre site, containing about 120 Mississippian culture mounds, that was the largest city of its time in North America, covering land on both sides of the Mississippi River near St. Louis, MO. Its main feature, Monks Mound, was named after a monastery built on its top during French occupation of the area. At 16-acres, the mound has a base larger than the Great Pyramid of Egypt, and is also the biggest man-made

Ariel View of Cahokia Mound

prehistoric structure in North America, dwarfed only by the pyramids at the Cholula and Teotihuacan. It is, however, the largest earthen structure in the world.

More recently, speculation on the purpose of this site has seemed to focus on its use as a possible ancient observatory, since a number of circular arrays have been found supporting this theory. The largest of these is over 400 feet across and was believed to have used wooden posts in 48 strategically placed holes to calculate solstices, equinoxes and even eclipses. It's an "American Woodhenge," declared Warren L. Witty, an archae-astronomer that has studied the site extensively.

What is probably most unusual about Cahokia is that we have almost no idea who the so-called Cahokians might have been, what language they spoke, or why and how they disappeared. The entire complex has Aztec and Mayan overtones, including its pyramidal structures and obligatory temples and sub-structures. But in fact, according to "official archaeology" no artifacts from Central American cultures has ever been found here, and therefore they don't fit with what "officially" should be this far north.

BEEHIVE CAVES

One of New England's infamous "Beehive Caves" can be found in Pelham, Massachusetts, on a private cemetery that has been in the Smith family for generations. The entrance to this igloo-like structure is barely visible from above ground. Below ground the interior broadens out into about a four-foot beehive structure made from mortarless dry masonry. Another "Beehive," this one free-standing and above ground, can be found on private land, near the town of Upton, Massachusetts. The entrance to this one is only about four feet high but has a 14-foot long entryway. As usual, authorities label such structures as "Colonial Root Cellars."

Another "Beehive Cave" can be found dug into the hill near Wendell, Massachusetts. This one is a little more accessible than the Pelham site mentioned above. In spite of it being a little smaller, three and a half feet in height instead of four feet, than Pelham, it does have features which are of more interest. There is also a crude monolith in the area with what appears to be a monk sitting inside a beehive inscribed on its surface, and was said to have been carved about 900 years ago. Centuries ago, the Culdee monks of Scotland and Ireland built similar structures, which has led to a theory about the beehive structures being alchemist's lairs for fugitive Irish monks. And of course, the official "colonial root cellar" or "steambath for

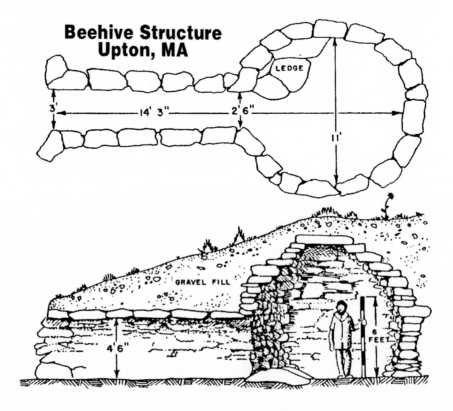

Beehive Structure Upton, MA

Indians" theories have predominated, but must be abandoned when compared to the beehive structures found throughout the North America. In fact, strikingly similar beehive-like structures have been found as far south as Central America.

AMERICA'S STONEHENGE

Probably one of America's most popular ancient sites is Mystery Hill, in North Salem, New Hampshire, which has come to be called America's Stonehenge. Spread across the 20-acre hilltop and woodland site are a number of unusual structures and foundations, including an assumed sacrificial slab, site lines for an ancient observatory, a deep "well" where non-native quartz crystals have been found, and the presence of dolmens and domed "beehive" structures similar to those found elsewhere in America.

There are a series of overlapping stone slabs, some as large as 20 tons, which form an arrangement of about 22 tunnels and enclosures on top of Pattee's Hill. The site may have been built as part of an extension of a natural cave system present in the hill. Several of the structures have apparent astronomical alignments. For instance, on the stone named the "Winter Solstice Monolith," the suns rays cut a direct line across the supposed sacrificial altar on December 21, the first day of Winter. On some of the structures on this site there are inscriptions that resemble those used by Phoenicians, including the design of a double-ax, or labrys, which has been associated with the early Mediterranean civilization of Crete. There is a shaft at the east end of the complex that is about 18-feet deep. In the bottom of this pit were found extraordinary bunches of quartz crystals that do not occur naturally anywhere near here.

Mystery Hill is probably most unusual in that it is characteristically unlike nearly every other ancient site in North America. Its megalithic building style is much more akin to ancient Irish and Scottish building sites than to anything found in America's past. An amateur archaeologist from Hartford, Connecticut, William B. Goodwing, believed that the Mystery Hill Complex was the relic of Irland-it-Mikla, the "Great Ireland" mentioned in Norse mariner legends. He suggested that the Culdee monks from Ireland had built the megalith after fleeing the Norse across the Atlantic, in the 9th century. Of course, the assertion of expert "professionals" is that the entire complex was built by a settler named Jonathan Pattee as a spare-time project, either that or they were constructed as "root cellars," take your pick.

THE MIMA MOUNDS

There are many unusual prostrate mounds in the remote prairie area northwest of Chehalis, Washington. The "Mima Mounds," as they are known, estimated at one time to be close to a million in number, at places reach a density of 10,000 per square mile. The largest mounds are about seven feet high and anywhere from 6 to 70 feet in diameter, and more than commonly than not, almost perfectly hemispherical.

The mounds are made mostly from gravel, with many containing large boulders, and some having a black silt foundation extending about a foot into the ground. Some locations have what appears to be cobblestones between the mounds, whereas other areas have an amalgam of gravel and silt. Early settlers assumed the mounds contained burials of some kind, as the Chinook Indian word for death is Mima, and yet, no Indian legends of the area are known.

**Mima Mounds
Chehalis, WA**

WASHINGTON STATE TRAVEL PHOTO

No human remains or artifacts of any kind have been found in any of the mounds excavated thus far. Apparently, the mounds may still be increasing in size, since old-timers in the area report that year-by-year they are slowly growing.

ANCIENT SETTLEMENTS

There is a great deal of evidence that entire parts of the Midwest, including parts of Iowa, Minnesota, and Wisconsin, were thoroughly submerged in an ice-melt ocean at the end of the last ice age. There is also consider-able proof that the area had been settled by what appear to be a Viking-like people centuries, and even millennia, before what the "authorities" will admit. Ships were brought in on the ancient shorelines and settlements were built. Various shoreline levels are evident throughout the area, most likely as a result of both slow drainage of the inland sea over time, and geological instability that caused entire regions to subside and change water levels.

Many of the stones and boulders along this shoreline were inevitably used as "mooring stones" to anchor boats or fly ceremonial or territorial flags. Invariably, these obvious mooring holes have been labeled as "blasting holes" by those responsible for informing the public of their archaeological significance, thus many have been entirely destroyed. In many cases, the sites were used as not only as boat docks, but lodging, ceremonial purposes, funerary burials, and for storage. Using sophisticated electromagnetic instruments, researchers have been able to locate the outline of structures, including longboats, beneath the ground at many sites. (See Orval D. Friedrich's books on early Vikings in the New World in the bibliography.)

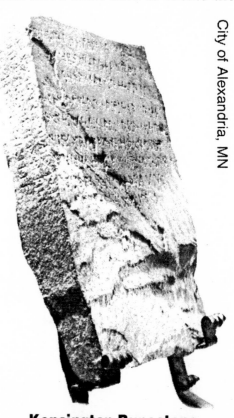

City of Alexandria, MN

Since we're on the subject of Vikings, let's talk about a large runestone, resembling a Viking ballast stone, that was found near Kensington, Minnesota, by a farmer named Olaf Ohman. The "Kensington Runestone," as it is

Kensington Runestone

known, weighs 202 pounds and measures 6 inches thick, 16 inches wide, and 31 inches long. On November 8th, 1898, Ohman claims he was trying to remove a 40-year-old aspen tree from his property and when it finally came up the monolith was tangled in its roots. This would seem to indicate that it had been inscribed long before Ohman found it, since he was just settling the land. After he found it, and local authorities showed little interest in it, he used it as a doorstep outside of a farm building. Luckily for us, he placed it face down.

A number of years had passed, and a student from the University of Wisconsin, Hjalmar Holand, heard of the stone. When he first asked to purchase it, Ohman wanted ten dollars, but the young student could only afford five, so Ohman just gave him the stone. Holand was then able to make what appears to be an accurate translation (without the punctuation) in 1909:

**Olof Ohman • November 1896
Story of 32 Scandinavians in 1362 C.E.**

"8 Goths and 22 Norwegians on exploration journey from Vineland round about the west. We had camp by [a lake with] 2 skerries 1 days journey north from this stone. We were [out] and fished one day. After we came home [found] 10 red with blood and dead. AV[e] M[aria]. Save [us] from evil."

And along the edge of the stone was inscribed: "Have 10 of [our party] by the sea to look after our ships. 14 days journey from this island. Year 1362."

It should be mentioned that some authorities believed that the stone had been forged by Ohman, but if that is indeed the case, he most surely did not profit from it. There have been a number of books that have written about the Kensington Runestone. The stone itself can still be found, eminently displayed, in the city of Alexandria, Minnesota.

ROCK LAKE

There has been a number of good books written on the mysteries beneath Rock Lake. It has an interesting history, in that inventor Max Gene Nohl tested a revolutionary innovation in this small Wisconsin lake that would forever change underwater exploration. The year was 1937 and Nohl had been interested in the Rock Lake mystery since pilot Dr. Fayette Morgan reported seeing underwater structures the previous year. He decided to field-test his Self Contained Underwater Breathing Apparatus, better known these days as S.C.U.B.A. gear, to try and confirm the report. He claims to have found a conical rock pyramid submerged in about 40 feet of water measuring about 29 feet high with an 18-foot wide base.

In more recent times, a number of other underwater structures have been discovered in this lake which resemble other pyramid-like constructions found throughout

North America. Though currently unconfirmed, one of the largest underwater structures was said to measure about 50 feet by 70 feet by 25 feet. Some of the smaller structures have square corners formed from straight edges. There is evidence that smoothly-mortared stones were used in some of the pyramids, and broken clam shells and split bones were found near others, similar to articles found near Aztalan.

THE DEVIL'S PLAYGROUND

This one really doesn't fit into any other category, but it is so very strange that it had to be included. Bizarre things are going on at a place called Racetrack Playa, also known as the Devil's Playground. In this isolated valley of the Cottonwood Mountains, at the northwest edge of Death Valley, there is an inexplicable phenomena of countless boulders, some weighing up to 600 pounds, that are being mysteriously slid across the desert floor. Measurements have shown that everything from small pebbles to large boulders are affected. The grooves range in width from a few inches to 12 feet and in length from 34 feet to more than 1,200 feet, with depths ranging from inconsequential to an inch or more.

Many of the furrows are straight, while others are curved, irregular, angular, zigzag, or in some cases a closed loop. Other phenomena of a similar nature can be found at McKittric, California; Bonnie Clair, Nevada; Nelson, Nevada; and Laguna Chapala, Baja California, Mexico. While some theories speculate that a geo-magnetic anomaly, involving a dense mass of underlying strata and the forces exerted by the rotation of the Earth are responsible, the "official" explanation is that the rocks are pushed over the frozen surface of the "dry lake" bed by strong winds.

CONCLUSION

There have been many unusual and puzzling artifacts that have been unearthed, or otherwise discovered, that do not fit into conventional theories of our geologic and historical past. While the entries in this short, if at times convoluted, report are for the most part from the United States, there are many more anomalous artifacts and archaeological evidence from sites worldwide. For those not familiar with some of the more sensational evidence that represents the earth's true history a few of the top-runners are outlined below.

Dropa Stone

The discovery of the Dropa Stones back in 1938 on an archeological expedition led by Dr. Chi Pu Tei of China probably tops the list of things everyone should know about. The "stones" were found buried beneath millennia of dust in caves in the Baian-Kara-Ula mountains. Numbering several hundred stones in all, each disk measured about nine inches in diameter and had a circle cut into the center, and spiral grooves etched into the surface, like an ancient phonograph record. Artifacts found with the stone disks have been dated to about 10,000 to 12,000 years ago. Small hieroglyphics were found in the grooves that, when translated, tell of an extraordinary story of extraterrestrials, who called themselves the Dropa, who had crash-landed in the mountains of China. Reports indicate that, in some of the caves, along with the disks, were discovered the remains of the Dropa, or their descendents, and that they may have, in fact, been Chinese.

A lot of interesting technology was being developed in the world 2,000 years ago. The predecessor of a modern, everyday item, found in nearly every retail store in the world, was discovered in the ruins of a Parthian village, in what is today

Remains of Baghdad Battery

modern-day Iraq. The "Baghdad Battery," as it has been called, is composed of a clay jar that is five and half inches high and contains a copper cylinder that was held in place by asphalt. Inside the copper tube was a rod made of disintegrating iron. All that was needed to produce electricity was an electrolytic alkaline or acidic solution. It is believed the instrument was used for electroplating with gold. The last known location of this incredible object was a museum in Baghdad.

To the northwest of Crete lies the small island of Antikythera, an out-of-the-way place in the Mediterranean Sea. In the year 1900, sponge divers discovered a shipwreck dating from before

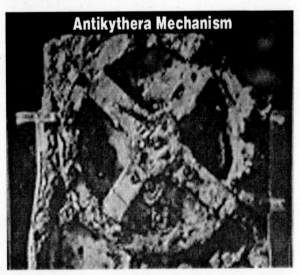

Antikythera Mechanism

the time of Christ in the shallow shores of this island. The ship's cargo of marble and bronze statues was subsequently salvaged from the site, and among the treasures was a corroded piece of bronze. Further inspection revealed that the artifact was made from a number of gears and wheels, and it was thought to be an astronomer's tool known as an astrolabe. The complexity and sophistication of the differential gears became apparent after an X-ray was taken of the object, revealing a degree of workmanship not possible until the 16th century.

Antikythera Mechanism, Dated Approximately 80 B.C.E.

Writing on the case of the object indicates it was manufactured in the year 80 B.C.E.

Grooved Stone South Africa

There are other mysterious stones as well. For nearly 40 years there have been reports from mine workers of unusual stone spheres, about an inch in diameter and scored with three parallel lines around the center, that are being dug up from mines in South Africa. The "grooved spheres" come in two types, one is of a hard blue metal with specks of white, while others have been hollowed out and filled with a white spongy material. The purpose or origin of the spheres are unknown, the rock from which they are being accidentally mined is Precambrian, dating to at least 2.8 billion years old.

On the other end of the "sphere" spectrum we find the giant stone balls of Costa Rica. In the 1930s, while cutting and burning their way through an impenetrable forest workers discovered a number of stone balls of various sizes, that were nearly perfectly spherical. The largest of the spheres is eight feet in diameter and weighs an incredible 16 tons. Are they man-made? It would appear so, but even the experts are puzzled as to their origin and purpose.

And then there's the scale models of ancient aircraft that have been found. Two cases come to mind: the solid golden delta-winged "ship" found in Central America, thought to have been a child's toy over a thousand years ago, though gold was only used as a tribute to the gods in that culture. And in Egypt, where a wooden model of an airplane, six inches in length, complete with wings, a tail, and fuselage was discovered in a tomb in Saqquara in 1898. Engineers believe the objects are aerodynamically feasible, or that both designs could fly. Of special interest is that these objects both had vertical stabilizers (the upraised tail section), something that birds do not have and so we would not expect to see had their inventors not experimented with flight.

There is a term, originally coined by Charles Fort, that is used in cryptoarchaeological circles called an OOPART, or Out-Of-Place-Artifact. The term can be applied to a good number of the artifacts that fit the description in this exposé. Here are a few more OOPARTs that fall into the "last but not least" category. A number of semi-ovoid metallic tubes have been found in chalk from the

Cretaceous age, ending 65 million years ago, at a mine in France. And in a report, from an unknown location in 1885, a perfect metal cube was found when breaking apart a chunk of coal. It had obviously been worked by human hands. And in 1912, workers preparing coal for an electric plant broke apart a large lump of coal and discovered an iron pot. Who knows what other mysteries lie in our hidden past.

So we have a few problems to resolve at this point. One scenario is that human beings have been around much longer than is generally accepted, and that we're only just now "rediscovering" our prehistoric past. Scenario number two, that would explain many of the strange and unusual artifacts described herein, is that there have been one or more advanced civilizations with a presence here on earth in the distant past that have since left, been destroyed, or died out. The question remains as to where these "other" cultures, if they existed, may have come from, or why they were here. We must also ask whether those cultures would have resembled our own or had been inhabited by human-like beings. Either way, something unusual has been going on.

For those of us who have done serious investigation on the subject of UFOs, and in particular ancient astronauts theories, it becomes apparent that the UFO phenomenon has been with us for at least the last several thousand years, and possibly much longer. Some researchers have speculated that that these ancient visitors may be responsible for our very existence. We won't take it quite that far this time. But what if there have been extraterrestrial visits to Earth for the past 2 or 3 billion years, as some of the evidence suggests? We may be just "one stop" on an intergalactic route of the gods.

77

It is a strange world we live in, and it sure is nice to be part of it. Thank you for joining us on our brief journey in exploring the enigmatic mysteries and anomalous artifacts of North America.

For information on subsequent volumes, updated news, additional images and text not included in this article due to space limitations please visit www.lostartsmedia.com and follow the appropriate link.

Only puny secrets need protection.
Big discoveries are protected by public incredulity.

–Marshall McLuhan and Barrington Nevitt

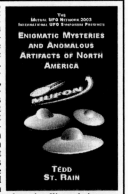

INDIVIDUAL WORKS CITED

"Another Strange Mine," *Info Journal* (International Fortean Organization, College Park, MD), no. 11, September 1973, p. 25.

F. A. Barnes, "The Case of the Bones in Stone," *Desert* magazine, February 1975, pp. 36-39.

Charles M. Boland, "They All Discovered America," p. 61.

Dorothy P Dansie, "John T. Reid's Case for the Redheaded Giants," *Nevada Historical Society Quarterly*, Fall 1975, pp. 153-167. Also pp 131-132.

Andrew E. Douglass, "Ancient Canals on the South-West Coast of Florida," *American Antiquarian*, vol. 7 (1885), pp. 277-285.

William E. DuBois, "On a Quasi Coin Reported Found in a Boring in Illinois," *Proceedings of the American Philosophical Society*, vol. 12, no. 86, 01 Dec 1871, pp. 224-228.

Hal Eberhart, "The Cogged Stones of Southern California," *American Antiquity*, vol. 26, no. 3, (1961), pp. 361-370.

John Green, "Fossil Tracks at Glen Rose," *Pursuit*, no. 36, Fall 1976, pp. 83-85.

Ronald L. Ives, "The Cochran Coke Ovens," *Journal of Arizona History*, Summer 1972, pp 73-81.

Allan O. Kelley, "Erratic Boulders on Point Loma," *Scientists Forum*, vol. 1, part 3, January 1971, Escondido, CA, pp. 80-81.

Robert R. Lyman, Forbidden Land as cited in "Giant Skeletons," *Pursuit*, vol. 6 no. 3, July 1973, pp 69-70.

O. C. Marsh, "Footprints in Nevada," *American Journal of Science*, vol. 126 (Jul-Dec 1883), pp. 139-140.

"Nevada's Red-Headed People Eaters," *INFO Journal*, no. 8, Winter-Spring 1972, pp 28-29.

Stephen D. Peet, "A Map of Emblematic Mounds...," *American Antiquarian*, vol. 11 March 1889, pp. 73ff.

A. L. Rawson, "The Ancient Inscription on a Wall at Chatata, Tennessee," *Transactions of the New York Academy of Science*, vol. 11, 09 Nov 1891, pp. 26-28.

"Remains of Vanished Giants Found in State," *Indianapolis News*, 10 Nov 1975.

E. B. Renaud, "Indian Enclosures of Colorado and New Mexico," (unpublished monograph of the Department of Anthropology), University of Denver, 1942

"Where Did All the Copper Go?" *INFO Journal*, No. 7 (Fall-Winter 1970), pp. 26-28.

OTHER WORKS CITED (BY STATE)

Crittenden, Arizona, *Deseret Weekly*, Salt Lake City, 14 Mar 1891.

Olancha, California, *INFO Journal*, No 4 (Spring 1969). pp 4-13.

Mauna Kea Volcano, Hawaii, *INFO Journal*, no. 7 (Fall/Winter 1970), p. 48.

Nampa, Idaho, *Proceedings of the Boston Society of Natural History*, vol. 24, pp 426ff. Also *Scribner's Magazine*, Feb 1890, pp. 235ff.

Rockcastle County, Kentucky, *New York Times*, 20 Jan 1938, p. 25.

Dorchester, Massachusetts, *Scientific American*, 1851.

Chatfield and Clearwater Minnesota, St. Paul *Pioneer*, 23 May 1883; 29 Jun 1888. Also St. Paul *Globe*, 12 Aug 1895.

Billings, Montana, The *Casper* (Wyoming) *Star-Tribune*, July 22nd and 24th, 1979.

—, The *Casper* (Wyoming) *Tribune Herald*, October 22, 1932.

—, *Carbon Country* (Montana) *News*, 11 Nov 1926, p. 5.

RECOMMENDED READING
AND AUTHORS CITED

Ancient American Magazine, www.ancientamerican.com

Charles Berlitz, World of Strange Phenomenon, Fawcett, NY, 1988.

Jim Brandon, Weird America, E.P. Dutton, NY, 1978.

David Hatcher Childress, Lost Cities of North and Central America, Adventures Unlimited Press, Kempton, IL, 1992.

Loren Coleman, Mysterious America, Faber & Faber, Inc., Boston, MA, 1983.

—, Curious Encounters, Faber & Faber, Boston, MA, 1985.

William R. Corliss, compiler, Strange Artifacts: A Sourcebook on Ancient Man, The Sourcebook Project, Glen Arm, Maryland, 1976 (from a series of source-books on unusual phenomenon).

Michael Cremo, Forbidden Archeology, Bhaktivedanta Book Publishing, Los Angeles, 1993.

—, Forbidden Archeology's Impact, Bhaktivedanta Book Publishing, Los Angeles, 1998.

Michael Cremo and Richard Thompson, The Hidden History of the Human Race. Govardhan Hill Publishing, Badger CA, 1994.

Frank Edwards, Stranger than Science, Ace Books, NY, 1959.

Barry Fell, America B.C., Demeter Press, NY, 1976.

Charles Fort, The Complete Books of Charles Fort, Dover, NY, 1976.

Neil Freer, God Games: What Do You Do Forever?, The Book Tree, San Diego, CA, 1 (800) 700-TREE, 1999.

—, Breaking the Godspell, The Book Tree, San Diego, CA, 1 (800) 700-TREE, 1987, 2000.

Orval Friedrich, Vikings Ho!, Self-published, 1996.

—, Vikings in the New World, Self-published, 1996.

Laurence Gardner, Bloodline of the Holy Grail, 1997.

—, Genesis of the Grail Kings, 2000.

—, Realm of the Ring Lords: The Myth and Magic of the Grail Quest, 2000.

Orville L. Hope, 6000 Years of Seafaring, Hope Press, Gastonia, NC, 1983.

Frank Joseph, Sacred Sites: A Guidebook to Sacred Centers and Mysterious Places in the United States, Llewellyn Publications, 1992.

— (edited by), Sacred Sites of the West: A Guide to Mystical Centers, Hancock House Publishers, 1997.

Brad Olsen, Sacred Places: 101 Spiritual Sites Around the World, Consortium of Collective Consciousness, 2000.

Lloyd Pye, Everything You Know Is Wrong - Book One: Human Origins, Adamu Press, iUniverse, 1998.

Salvatore M. Trento, Field Guide to Mysterious Places of the West, Pruett Publishing Company, 1994.

—, Field Guide to Mysterious Places of Eastern North America, Henry Holt and Company, Inc., 1997.

—, Field Guide to Mysterious Places of the Pacific Coast, Henry Holt and Company, Inc., 1997.

Zecharia Sitchin, The Twelfth Planet, Avon Books, NY, 1976.

—, Stairway to Heaven, Avon Books, NY, 1980.

—, The Wars of Gods and Men, Avon Books, NY, 1985.

—, The Lost Realms, Avon Books, NY, 1990.

—, Genesis Revisited: Is Modern Science Catching Up with Ancient Knowledge, Avon Books, NY, 1991.

Gunnar Thompson, American Discovery, 1992.

Immanuel Velikovski, Worlds in Collision, Dell Publishing Co., NY, 1950.

FINIS

Tédd St. Rain has had an intense interest in all things preternatural since childhood, and has been actively researching the mysterious, the metaphysical and the mythical for almost 20 years now. Born and raised in Long Beach, CA, an author, lecturer, and videographer, he has traveled the world extensively investigating the world's ancient mysteries and enigmas. He is the owner of Lost Arts Media that publishes, markets and distributes a variety of products and services.

Tédd St Rain

CALL FOR OUR FREE CATALOG. The mission of Lost Arts Media is to provide fascinating and educational books, videos and multimedia products to help inform, enlighten and inspire humanity. We are also involved in document research, video production, e-books, DVD authoring, broadcasting, screenwriting, conference promotion, online services, amongst many other creative endeavors. Call to have your conference or lecture videotaped and/or distributed. We carry Books, Booklets, Audio, CD, Video, DVD, Music, Multimedia and other products on Ancient History, Anthropology, Archaeology, Human Origins, the Paranormal, and so much more. In compiling a research information archive from various sources, including research and public libraries, the internet, newspapers, journals, magazines, newsletters, press releases, and product literature, St. Rain has amassed nearly 20,000 pages of hard copy documentation on a variety of topics. Tédd St. Rain is available for radio, TV, and public speaking engagements on any number of subjects. He may be contacted through Lost Arts Media • P.O. Box 15026 • Long Beach, CA 90815 • 1 (800) 952-LOST • 1 (562) 596-ARTS • lostartsmedia@yahoo.com • www.lostartsmedia.com

BOOK, VIDEO and RESEARCH ARCHIVE
CALL FOR OUR FREE CATALOG

www.lostartsmedia.com • 1 (800) 952-LOST

Ancient Mysteries of North America, by Tédd St. Rain. This in-depth slide presentations, which is based on his forthcoming book *Mystery of America*, outlines some of the most perplexing ancient mysteries and other anomalies that have been found in North America. Explore the evidence for Arabian, Celtic, Chinese, Egyptian, Greco-Roman, Hindu, Irish, Mesopotamian, Minoan, Nordic, Pacific Islander, Phoenician, Viking, Welsh, and West African voyages to the New World. Other topics include runestones and tablets found in the East; pre-historic mines near Lake Superior; Roman relics found in Arizona; enigmatic bee-hive structures, ancient coins unearthed in the Midwest; elephant slabs found in New Mexico; ground and rock petroglyphs in the Southwest; Egyptian hieroglyphics and Chinese characters; drawings of feathered serpents in Illinois; ancient footprints fossilized in rock; mound builders and their burial mounds; a 14-inch mummy found in Wyoming; human teeth found in coal deposits; red-headed giants that lived in Nevada; underground cities in the Grand Canyon; evidence for an advanced civilization; and many more anomalous finds discovered in North America. AMNA-01a • 110 min Audio Tape • $12.00 / AMNA-01 • 110 min VHS Video Tape • $19.95 Inquire on availability of other videos in St. Rain's *"Mystery of the World"* series.

Remote Viewing Training Sessions

Remote Viewing Training Sessions: Discovering Your Intuition, with Prudence Calabrese and TransDimensional Systems. Prudence Calabrese is the Director of TransDimensional Systems, www.largeruniverse.com, which provides information solutions to government, corporations and individuals using an array of services including remote viewing, knosomatics, intuitive counseling, technology transfer, consciousness mapping, physical profiling and other techniques. Prudence has been teaching people to remote view since 1996. She takes the scientific approach to the study of remote viewing and has developed methods and techniques that go far beyond the restrictive, protocol-based traditional remote viewing first developed over a generation ago at Stanford Research Institute. This seven-part, 13 hour, video program includes training in Basic Remote Viewing and Knosomatics, the Collector, Use of the Matrix and Advanced Post-Matrix Exercises. Included as a bonus is a discussion and explanation of techniques in Remote Healing and use of Remote Viewing for everyday purposes and career choices. Also covered is a live remote viewing and Knosomatics demonstration by Prudence and her team of professional remote viewers as presented for the London Sunday Times and HBO. This series takes the new Remote Viewer all the way through the Basic Training required to successfully remote view. Actual in-class results are shared, sessions are examined and the entire process is revealed. Join Prudence Calabrese and her staff as she leads another class into the unknown world and the Larger Universe. It's all here for you to watch, enjoy and learn. RVT-00a • 13 Hours on 7 Audio Tapes • $55.00 postpaid / RVT-00 • 13 Hours on 7 VHS Video Tapes • $110.00 postpaid / Introduction only • RVT-01 • 2 hour VHS Video Tape • $19.95

The New Living Expo 2003

MARS AND VENUS ON A DIET, with John Gray. John Gray presents the concepts and invaluable practices from his new book The Mars and Venus Diet and Exercise Solution, revealing little-known information regarding how diet, exercise and communication skills combine to affect the production of healthy brain chemicals. Exploring issues not commonly known or expressed in other books and programs, you will gain insight to understand little known gender insights. This special worskshop presents the basic information for understanding nutrition, exercise, brain chemistry, sex hormones and stress management. In addition, this tape explains how necessary relationship skills will successfully stimulate the healthy production of brain chemicals. Once you have all the pieces of the puzzle in front of you, suddenly it all fits neatly together and you realize why diets, exercise programs or relationships may have failed in the past. NLE-01a • 113 min Audio • $12.00 / NLE-01 • 113 min Video • $19.95

THE POWER OF FOCUS, with Jack Canfield. Jack Canfield is a skilled success coach, human potential trainer and the author of 60 books and ten audio programs including The Success Principles, Self-Esteem and Peak Performance, The Power of Focus and the best-selling Chicken Soup for the Soul series with over 80 million copies in print. Based on his best-selling book, The Power of Focus: How to Hit Your Business, Personal and Financial Targets with Absolute Certainty, this presentation will share the secrets of how to double your income and double your time off in three years or less. Learn how to create more income, greater results, more time off and greater balance in your life. It's all possible. Jack will draw upon his 30 years of teaching experience and coaching people to achieve results. NLE-02a • 120 min Audio • $12.00 / NLE-02 • 125 min Video • $24.95

A REVOLUTIONARY NEW PROGRAM FOR WEIGHT LOSS, GREATER HEALTH AND EMOTIONAL HAPPINESS, with Jack Canfield and John Gray. Two legends of the health and relationship well-being genre – Jack Canfield and John Gray – discuss a revolutionary new weight-loss program that they have both benefited from and are now endorsing. Learn how with the right nutrition and exercise you and those you love can quickly, easily and effortlessly lose weight whenever you want and reap many other side benefits in your emotional and relational life as well. Jack Canfield lost 33 pounds in 35 days on this program, John Gray lost 15 pounds in 20 days, and others, have lost as much as 110 pounds in 5 months. Jack Canfield has collected over 60 of these success stories in his new book Chicken Soup for the Healthy Soul and John Gray writes about the program in his newest book The Mars and Venus Diet and Exercise Solution. NLE-03a • 2 90 min Audios • $20.00 / NLE-03 • 134 min Video • $24.95

THE TRIBULATION AND THE EXODUS GENERATION, with Sean David Morton. "Sean David Morton is the real thing. A truly brilliant and witty modern day prophet. In fact he has become America's prophet. A true voice for all that lies ahead. I joke that he has more "hits" than Mark McGuire, Barry Bonds, the Sopranos or the Russian Mafia! Time and again, he has given exact dates for major world events. He has been so deadly accurate that it frightens. His predictions on my show been nothing short of astounding!" –Art Bell. Sean achieved national recognition when his expeditions to Area 51 made front-page news in the Los Angeles Times. Currently Sean is the director of the Prophecy Research Institute and since 1993 has published the Delphi Associates Newsletter. He continues to work in the TV and film industry as a writer and producer. He has gained worldwide fame and recognition for his incredibly accurate predictions given in his newsletter, Art Bell's radio show and his many TV appearances. Using his unique abilities as an Earth sensitive, and with information from his spiritual travels to our future, Sean will lay out the monumental time-line leading through the Great Exodus, this Age of Heroes and on into the Messianic Age. Specifics to be covered are the mark of the beast, the fate of America, Earth changes, economic forecasts, the presidency, the last great war and the coming messiah. NLE-04a • 2 90 min Audios • $20.00 / NLE-04v • 135 min Video • $24.95

SAVED BY THE LIGHT, with Dannion Brinkley. Dannion Brinkley is the international best-selling author of Saved by the Light and At Peace With The Light. Saved By The Light was made into a television motion picture seen in over 60 countries. His amazing story has earned him appearances on Oprah, Larry King Live, CNN World News, Unsolved Mysteries, the BBC and many other television, radio and internet programs. Dannion is well known for his ability to survive against seemingly impossible odds including enduring two lightning strikes, open heart surgery, brain surgery and a massive grand mal seizure. After three NDEs (near death experiences) many concur that Brinkley is a walking miracle. Brinkley has taught millions not to fear the presently held concept of dying. For as a result of his journeys to the 'other side' and back again, Dannion brings to the forefront the wondrous truth that there is indeed no such thing as death. His light-hearted and uproariously humorous delivery makes this workshop presentation informative and entertaining. NLE-05a • 105 min Audio • $12.00 / NLE-05v • 105 min Video • $19.95

PERFECT HEALTH: AN INTRODUCTION TO THE WORK OF DEEPAK CHOPRA, MD, with Leanne Backer and Bea Sochor. Leanne Backer is the lead educator and executive chef for the Chopra Center for Well Being. Join her and Chopra instructor Bea Sochor as they lead you through an introduction to the world-renowned work of Dr. Deepak Chopra. The presentation begins with a primordial sound mediation, leading into an overview of the principles of Ayurveda and nutrition. Also includes a question and answer period. This tape provides an overview of how these principles can lead to a balanced lifestyle and perfect health. NLE-06a • 85 min Audio • $12.00 / NLE-06v • 85 min Video • $19.95

COMPASSION, DNA and PSYCHIC ABILITY, with Jelaila Starr. Jelaila Starr is an acclaimed Niburuan messenger, channel, teacher, counselor and author of We Are the Nibiruans. She touches the hearts of people around the world inspiring hope and understanding through her teachings of compassion. In this presentation she explains how to regain our psychic abilities, why it seems so difficult to do, what's the secret, and what the connection between our DNA, psychic ability and compassion? Join Jelaila as she reveals the secret "inner technology" locked within our DNA that not only restores our psychic abilities, but also returns us to full consciousness, enabling us to ascend and create the world we desire. NLE-07a • 62 min Audio • $12.00 / NLE-07v • 62 min Video • $19.95

THE PATH OF RELATIONSHIP, with Shakti Gawain. Shakti Gawain is a pioneer in the field of personal growth. Her many best-selling books include Creative Visualization, Living in the Light and The Path of Transformation. She discusses how our most important relationship is with ourselves, because it is the foundation for our life. All other relationships are mirrors which can help us become conscious, integrated beings. Discover how you can use your relationships as the most effective path to consciousness. Find out exactly how problem areas in your relationships reflect valuable lessons you need to learn so that you can experience more fulfilment and satisfaction in life. Some areas of discussion will include discovering why opposites attract, moving through fear of commitment, finding a life partner, communicating honestly and effectively, balancing closeness and independence, integrating our shadow side and developing true intimacy. NLE-08a • 111 min Audio • $12.00 / NLE-08v • 111 min Video • $19.95

BUDDHISM ON TURTLE ISLAND – ITS FIFTH RENAISSANCE, with Robert A. F. Thurman. Robert Thurman is a scholar, author, former Tibetan Buddhist mon, Director of Tibet House in New York City, and a close personal friend of His Holiness the 14th Dalai Lama. Professor Gadjun Nagao once put forth a theory about the fifth renaissance of Buddhism possibly occurring in America. It could happen! To ponder this, we must first consider what Buddhism is? A way of life? A philosophy? A religion? A meditative practice? Would its spread in America be a good thing? What could a practicing Buddhist do to help it along? Should followers of religions regard it with apprehension? Compete with it? Welcome it with open arms? These questions and more are answered in this sketch of a positive vision of the future of Buddhism in America. NLE-09a • 78 min Audio • $12.00 / NLE-09v • 78 min Video • $19.95

FROM CHAOS TO CREATION, with Jean Houston. Jean Houston is a prolific author and scholar. Among her many books are Public Like A Frog, The Hero and The Goddess, The Possible Human, the Search for the Beloved, Manual for the Peacemaker, amongst others. Sometimes the human species has been left with a challenge so huge and so singular as to seem more mythic than real. We currently live at the center of this challenge. What can consciousness, with its immense resources, bring to such a critical moment? We must seek deeper meaning to the great questions that have energized people to tap into the unknown. These aspects of ourselves, the engendering of a passion for the possible in our human and social development. In so doing, we discover ways of transcending and transforming. It is an extraordinary life that has the capacity to engage the world and make a difference. NLE-10a • 107 min Audio • $12.00 / NLE-10v • 107 min Video • $19.95

EROS, GENDER AND THE SACRED PANEL DISCUSSION, with Randy Conner, David Sparks, Xochipala Maes Valdez, Arisika Razak and Andrew Ramer. This powerful and important panel discussion about sexuality, spirituality and the LGBT community. What are the gifts and visions that this community brings to spiritual traditions? What are the roles that LGBT persons have played in religious and spiritual movements? How do we get past gender and preference and go to the depth of the human soul. This presentation explains all of this and more. Randy Conner, the moderator, is an educator and author of Encyclopedia of Queer Myths, Symbol and Spirit. David Sparks is an ethnomusicologist and writer. Xochipala Maes Valdez is a Yoruba Priest of Isa and Obatala. Arisika Razak is on the faculty of the California Institute of Integral Studies. Andrew Ramer is the author of Two Flutes Plays. Come join these experts as they discuss the sacred, gender and the spirit. NLE-11a • 75 min Audio • $12.00 / NLE-11v • 75 min Video • $19.95

UFOS: THE CURRENT CONVERSATION, with Robert Perala, Dr. Brian O'Leary, Ralph Steiner, Linda WIllets, Michael Horn and Mark Kimmel. Up until now, most of the focus on UFOs has been "is any of this real, and if it is real, where is the evidence?" Only by exposing the full truth around the UFO question can we get to the core reasons for the intense secrecy surrounding this issue and the potential use of a highly sophisticated technology for the betterment of our planet. Many researchers now realize that this deep rooted political, economic and social issue that transcends the mere notion that the totality of this experience revolves around hardware and sightings of craft. Only by discussing the full truth around the UFO question can we get to the core reasons for the intense secrecy surrounding this issue. Robert Perala, the moderator, is the author of Divine Blueprint, Brian O'Leary is a former NASA astronaut and scientist, Ralph Steiner is an independent producer and science journalist, Linda Willets is an assistant to Dr. Steven Greer and the Disclosure Project, Michael Horn represents the Billy Meier material and Mark Kimmel is the author of Trillium, a message of extraterrestrial and spiritual implications. Join this panel of experts as they discuss the mysteries of UFOs and extraterrestrial life. NLE-12a • 85 min Audio • $12.00 / NLE-12v • 85 min Video • $19.95

Signs of Destiny: Crop Circles and Sacred Geometry Conference 2002

EGYPT AND THE SCIENCE OF IMMORTALITY: Parts 1 and 2, with John Anthony West. Ancient Egypt was a one-issue civilization - its energies were entirely devoted to expressing and furthering its doctrine of Immortality. The number symbolism, the geometry of the temples, the fabulous architecture, art and sculpture, even the gods themselves, all played a role in this astonishing doctrine that fused science, art, religion and philosophy into a single, coherent Wisdom Teaching. Mere lectures do not allow enough time to broach this broad subject, but this 3-hour Institute provides a golden opportunity to explore Ancient Egypt's major aspects in depth, along with my latest research into how that system actually performed. This presentation is his Friday afternoon workshop. SIGNS-01a & 02a • 2 90 min Audios • $22.00 / SIGNS-01 and 02 • 2 90 min Videos • $39.95

THE GREAT SPHINX AND THE QUEST TO REWRITE HISTORY, with John Anthony West. A writer, scholar and Pythagorean from New York, John Anthony West is the author of "The Traveler's Key to Ancient Egypt" and "Seprent in the Sky: The High Wisdom of Ancient Egypt." The ancient Egyptians attributed their wisdom to an earlier age going back 36,000 years. John set out to test whether the Sphinx is older than its recognized date of 2,500 B.C. His finding provide the first hard evidence that an earlier civilization preceded Egypt's dynastic history. Today he's an authority on the "Symbolist" school of Egyptology, a view first proposed by French scholar-philosopher, R. A. Schwaller de Lubicz. In the Symbolist view, ancient Egyptian art and architecture disclose richer, more universal wisdom than conventional Egyptology has assumed. John Anthony West won an Emmy Award for his 1993 NBC Special Documentary, "The Mystery of the Sphinx," hosted by Charlton Heston. This presentation is his Saturday evening keynote address. For more information visit www.jawest.com SIGNS-03a • 2 70 min Audios • $19.95 / SIGNS-03 •139 min Video • $24.95

THE CROP CIRCLES PRIMARY MESSAGE, with Drunvalo Melchizedek. As a celebrated mystic and teacher, Drunvalo Melchizedek's life experience reads like and encyclopedia of breakthroughs in human endeavor. After having taking physics and art at UC Berkeley, he ventured out, and over the last 25 years has studied with over 70 masters from all belief systems and religious backgrounds. An accomplished speaker, he instinctively communicates what's in this heart, his personal warmth, his love for life in all forms and his deep compassion for humanity. His "Flower of Life" teachings and "Mer-ka-ba" meditation system have help thousands better understand their own history and life's work. An expert on Sacred Geometry, he has studied how Crop Circles manifest these ancient forms for a decade. For more information visit www.floweroflife.com SIGNS-04a • 118 min Audio • $12.00 / SIGNS-04 • 118 min Video • $19.95

SACRED GEOMETRY WORKSHOP, with Drunvalo Melchizedek. Drunvalo's information was given to him from 1972 through the 1980s by Thoth, best known as the Egyptian deity of inner wisdom pertaining to science, mathematics, and literature. Since the 1980s, Drunvalo has been presenting his Flower of Life Workshops (either personally or through his trained facilitators). His work has been spread to at least 40 countries, is taught in many languages (such as Spanish, Dutch, German, French, Japanese), and has deeply touched thousands of people around the globe. When the teachings of geometry are used to show the ancient truth that all life emerges from the same blueprint, we can clearly see that life springs from the same source – the intelligent, unconditionally loving creative force some call "God." When geometry is used to express and explore this great truth, a broader understanding of the universe unfolds until we can see that all aspects of reality become sacred. The ancients such as the Egyptians, Mayans, and others all knew this truth and incorporated sacred geometry teachings into their mystery schools as a way for anyone to begin to practically understand his or her personal relationship to "God" and the universe. In this presentation, Drunvalo speaks on the experience in his life that lead him on the path to the practice the flower of life teachings. A full two-hour presentation on the flower of life and sacred geometry. For more information visit www.floweroflife.com SIGNS-05a • 2 hour Audio • $12.00 / SIGNS-05 •118 min Video • $19.95

THE IMPORTANCE OF HOW AND WHEN THE CROP CIRCLE PHENOMENON BEGAN, with Colin Andrews. One of the earliest and best-known crop circle researchers and authors, Colin became involved in this mystery when, in 1983, he saw a quintuplet formation near his home in Andover, England. An electrical engineer by training, he was intrigued about what forces could create such perfect glyphs in crop fields. In 1989 he and Pat Delgado wrote "Circular Evidence," a best-seller, followed by "Crop Circles: The Latest Evidence," a year later. Colin founded Circles Phenomenon Research International (CPRI) and later moved to Connecticut. His scientific investigations have been widely recognized as models in the field and he has been featured in many crop circle documentaries. Recently, he has stated that while he considers many complex formations to be man-made, one cannot rule out unknown paranormal involvement in the rest. For more information visit www.cropcircleinfo.com SIGNS-06a • 92 min Audio • $12.00 / SIGNS-06 • 92 min Video • $19.95

THERMAL PLASMAS OF UNKNOWN ORIGIN: Hessdalen 2002, with Linda Moulton Howe. An Emmy-award winning investigative journalist and author, now living near Philadelphia, Linda was the creative genius behind the original "Sightings" TV Series. For several years she has provided millions of listeners with a weekly UFO update and summary at the beginning of the "Dreamland" radio show and has done numerous guest appearances on Art Bell's "Coast to Coast" late-night show. One of the most serious and respected investigators of the paranormal, her interests include alien abductions, animal mutilations, crop circles and ET contacts. She has This lecture focuses on here latest research into the mysterious plasma and glowing orb effects found in a remote valley in Hessdalen, Norway. She's working on a new documentary on the subject, visit www.earthfiles.com for more information. SIGNS-07a • 54 min Audio • $12.00 / SIGNS-07 • 54 min Video • $19.95

THE CIRCLES, THE SCIENCE AND AN EYEWITNESS ACCOUNT, with Nancy Talbott. Raised in Baltimore, Nancy studied psychology at Johns Hopkins and Harvard. After discovering the crop circle phenomenon in 1991, she worked with Michigan biophysicist Wm. C. Levengood and John Burke, organizing an international reporting and field-sampling network for Wm. Levengood's laboratory analysis. In 1999 she incorporated the BLT Research organization into a non-profit corporation, which she now heads, and received a Laurence Rockefeller grant. With this funding she has expanded the scope of crop circle research so that BLT Inc. team now includes scientific consultants from multiple disciplines. Having herself had both personal experiences and scientific training, Nancy has a unique perspective on this ongoing enigma. For more information visit www.bltresearch.com SIGNS-08a • 92 min Audio • $12.00 / SIGNS-08 • 92 min Video • $19.95

SCIENTIFIC ANALYSIS OF CROP CIRCLES: A Practical Guide, with Nancy Talbott. Nancy Talbott is president of BLT Research Team Inc., whose primary goal is the discovery and scientific documentation of physical changes induced in plants, soils and other materials at crop circle sites by the energy (or energy system) responsible for creating them and to determine, if possible, from these data the specific nature and source of these energies. Secondly, our intent is to publish these research results in peer-reviewed scientific journals and to disseminate this information to the general public. BLT Inc. is comprised of several hundred trained field-sampling personnel in the U.S., Canada and Europe who collect plant and soil samples at crop circle sites for analyses by a number of scientists (see "Professional Consultants") in various disciplines. The hard work of these field teams and their careful adherence to field-sampling protocols has contributed enormously to the on-going discoveries in the laboratory and the large database of factual information that now exists. This presentation outlines the basic research and results obtained so far, highlighting individual crop circle case studies from a number of countries. Slides of recent crop circles in North America and Europe are included, as well as anecdotal reports of associated strange phenomena encountered by personnel working in the fields each summer. For more information visit www.bltresearch.com SIGNS-09a • 108 min Audio • $12.00 / SIGNS-09 • 108 min Video • $19.95

FIELD OF DREAMS: Crop Circles in Canada, with Paul Anderson. A media writer and graphic designer by profession, Paul Anderson has had a life-long interest in future studies and alternative science. In 1990, he became fascinated with the visually-inspiring crop circle phenomenon. As the numbers of Canadian formations grew, he saw the need for an organized network of local researchers to study them scientifically. He help found the group that is now known as the "Canadian Crop Circle Research Network." It links researchers in seven Canadian provinces. As group coordinator, Paul maintains the CCCRN website, www.cccrn.com, and E-news service from his Vancouver, BC, office. SIGNS-10a • 68 min Audio • $12.00 / SIGNS-10 • 68 min Video • $19.95

GROWING CROP CIRCLE SEEDS FOR FOOD, with Steve Purkable. A gentleman farmer from Illinois, Steve Purkable became interested in crop circles in 1992 and built his first 3-D model of a formation in April, 1993. Since then he has made more than 400 models of different crop circles. In 1997, he came into possession of some crop circle wheat seeds and began a long-term study of their growth potential. His seventh generation of crop circle wheat plantings has recently matured. SIGNS-11a • 26 min Audio • $12.00 / SIGNS-11 • 26 min Video • $19.95

ENGLAND'S CROP CIRCLES OF 2002, with Francine Blake. A native of Montreal, Canada, Francine studied the Classics and Art. In 1969 she moved to London to continue her studies; there she married and Englishman. A student of Gurdjief's philosophy and Zen Buddhism, she discovered the crop circle phenomenon in 1987. In 1992, she and her family moved to Wiltshire where she helped found the Wiltshire branch of the "Center for Crop Circle Studies." The group became the "Wiltshire Crop Circle Study Group" in 1996. As its coordinator, Francine now edits "The Spiral," and organizes the Wiltshire Crop Circle Conference each summer. An accomplished painter, she learned digital photography for the group's annual calendar, the only one to feature color aerial photos of the current season. She feels most crop circles are "manifestations from other dimensions" and not mere human creations. SIGNS-12a • 115 min Audio • $12.00 / SIGNS-12 • 115 min Video • $19.95

CROP CIRCLES IN GERMANY: Amazing Recent Developments, with Andreas Mueller. As a student of graphic design at the School of Fine Arts and Design in Saarbrucken, Germany, Andreas Mueller became interested in the crop circle phenomenon for nearly 10 years. Since 1994 he has been investigating crop circles in both England and Germany. In 1994, he also founded the "International Crop Circle Archives," which has become one of the largest databases on this phenomenon with 4,000 records from 45 countries, covering five centuries. In 2001 he published "Kornkreise: Geometric, Phaenomene, Forshung," in German. His slide lecture will also feature photos taken by German photographer Frank Laumen. For more information visit www.invisiblecircle.de SIGNS-13a • 85 min Audio • $12.00 / SIGNS-13 • 85 min Video • $19.95

CROP CIRCLES REVEALED: A Spiritual Perspective, with Barbara Lamb. A licensed Psychotherapist in Claremont, CA, specializing in hypnotic regressions to remember past lives or alien contacts. Barbara has also been investigating crop circles since 1991. She recently co-authored "Crop Circles Revealed: Language of the Light Symbols," with channel Judith Moore. Barbara has stated her belief that the electromagnetic light and sound frequencies of each crop circle are mathematical and geometric formulas for the healing of our planet, for the evolution of our world and for the spiritual ascension of the human species. Barbara's unique perspective on the crop circle enigma even takes "human-made" formations into account as she feels they too are influenced by unseen forces whose ultimate purpose is both positive and spiritual. For more information visit www.blambms.com SIGNS-14a • 85 min Audio • $12.00 / SIGNS-14 • 85 min Video • $19.95

CROP CIRCLES 2001-2002: A Year of Surprises, with Dr. Chet Snow. An internationally-acclaimed author, lecturer, researcher and regression therapist, Chet Snow has degrees from Columbia University and Paris' Sorbonne. As the promoter of the "Signs of Destiny" conference, the third in a series of Earth Mysteries conventions, designed to study what has led our species and the planet to these special times of challenge and opportunity. In this lecture, Chet Snow will reveal the latest information on crop circles from the English countryside of the 2001-2002 season. For more information and to find out about future events visit www.chetsnow.com SIGNS-15a • 53 min Audio • $12.00 / SIGNS-15 • 53 min Video • $19.95

SIGNS OF DESTINY: Crop Circle and Sacred Geometry Conference 2002 - Tempe, Arizona. Complete conference set. SIGNS-92a • 22+ hours on 16 audio tapes • $120.00 • SIGNS-92 • 22+ hours on 15 videotapes • $225.00

New Science / Ancient Wisdom - 2000 Conference

THE COSMIC ORIGINS OF MAN, with Father Charles Moore. Father Charles Moore graduated from Stanford University with a degree in law, was admitted to the California Bar and then was elected District Attorney of Santa Cruz County in 1954. He was ordained a Roman Catholic Priest in 1964. Father Charlie is a local spiritual leader, historian and scholar who speaks about our history, spirituality, ancient cultures and modern society. His broad grasp on human nature, our origins, organized religions, legends and myths make this presentation a fascinating and informative exposé of our ancient political and religious practices. Learn about the "Theories of Knowledge" and the "100th Monkey Internet." With his incredible knowledge he gives new dimensions and deeper understandings to topics we thought we already knew. He has traveled extensively in search of the roots of religious practice. His quest has taken him to Britain, Europe, Alaska, Mexico, and India as well as he homelands of several Native American tribes where he has studied over a dozen languages. He shares with us his highly unconventional views about human genetic, religious and cultural origins. BACN-01a • 108 min Audio Tape • $12.00 / BACN-01 • 108 min VHS Video Tape • $19.95

21ST CENTURY VISIONS OF NOSTRADAMUS, with Dolores Cannon. Dolores Cannon is an internationally known specialist in the recovery and cataloging of "lost" knowledge through regression. Cannon is a regressive hypnotist specializing in past life recall, and she is fascinated by the details of history revealed by many of her subjects. Through her communication with Nostradamus, she has written three volumes of "conversations" which interpret almost 1000 prophecies of the 16th century seer. Her Nostradamus series is particularly interesting, as her subjects appear to have traveled through both time and space while in trance, and to have contacted the living Michel de Notredame, (Nostradamus) in his own time. Dolores Cannon is a warm and likable person. Working through several different subjects, Dolores was able to establish communication with the living Michel De Notredame better known as the prophet, Nostradamus. His revelations and their impact on our own time provide a fascinating look into a rarely discussed subject. BACN-02a • 92 min Audio Tape • $12.00 / BACN-02 • 92 min VHS Video Tape • $19.95

HUMAN RELATIONSHIPS WITH ETS, with Barbara Lamb. Barbara Lamb, a regular at our conferences and one of the nation's most experienced therapists working with UFO experiencers, suggests that either the numbers of experiencers are rising rapidly or more people are willing to talk publicly about such encounters. Barbara Lamb is a licensed Marriage and Family Therapist who specializes in doing regression therapy with extraterrestrial contactees and abductees. A former Executive Vice President of the Association for Past Life Research and Therapies, Lamb has trained many other psychotherapists and hypnotherapists. Ms. Lamb has worked with over 200 separate individuals who have come to her for clarity in regards to their ET contacts. Barbara is well known and highly respected for her work on an international level. This tape describes her experiences in hypnotherapy with regards to human relationships with extraterrestrials. She discusses ongoing human relationships with ETs and shows slides that she has just recently compiled. BACN-03a • 55 min Audio Tape • $12.00 / BACN-03 • 55 min VHS Video Tape • $19.95

ET RELATIONSHIPS PANEL, with Barbara Lamb, Pamela Stonebrooke, Eve Lorgen and Dolores Cannon. Barbara Lamb, a regular at our conferences and one of the nation's most experienced therapists working with UFO experiencers, suggests that either the numbers of experiencers are rising rapidly or more people are willing to talk publicly about such encounters. Pamela Stonebrooke, also known as the Intergalactic Diva, a professional singer in the Los Angeles area, is writing the story of her alien encounters. In her presentation, Pamela shares her encounters with her four Grey hybrid daughters, and openly discusses her experiences with the Reptilians. From terror and denial to awakening and expansion, Pamela proposes a metaphysical perspective of this phenomenon. Eve Lorgen's interest in the UFO phenomenon began early in life as a result of multiple witnessed UFO sightings with family members. She holds a Bachelor's degree in Biochemistry from San Francisco State University and a Master's degree in counseling Psychology. She provides insights from her recent book, The Alien Love Bite: Alien Interference in Human Love Relationships, which explores how alien beings may be orchestrating human love dramas for their own ends. Dolores Cannon has written several books on the prophecies of Nostradamus. On the panel, she shares information from her latest book, The Custodians, which discusses distorted time, screen memories and reasons for abductions. These experts have gathered to discuss the relationships between ETs and humans. BACN-04a • 80 min Audio Tape • $12.00 / BACN-04 • 80 min VHS Video Tape • $19.95

SCIENCE, POLITICS AND THE NEW MILLENNIUM, with Dr. Nick Begich. Best selling author and lecturer Dr. Nick Begich presents an overview of the HAARP (High Frequency Active Auroral Research Program) transmitter and antenna in Alaska. His countless years of research help to provide a glimpse of new technological achievements that can help better the environment and reshape mankind in the future. Pulling from an array of extensive documentation from government, academic and media sources, Begich is able explain the big picture in terms that anyone can understand. Nick Begich co-authored the book Angels Don't Play This HAARP: Advances in Tesla Technology, and wrote Towards a New Alchemy: The Millennium Science. His latest book Earth Rising - The Revolution: Toward a Thousand Years of Peace was co-authored with James Roderick in December 1999. He is also the editor of Earthpulse Flashpoints, a continuing new-science book series. On the eve of the 2000 presidential election, Nick discussed science and politics in the new millennium. He discussed differences between the two major parties and what is going behind the scenes. He also gave an update on the latest research activities including new technologies, health and earth science related issues. There was a citywide power loss shortly after Begich began his presentation, but through the use of a quickly replaced battery pack, only a few moments of this valuable presentation were lost. BACN-05a • 119 min Audio Tape • $12.00 / BACN-05 • 119 min VHS Video Tape • $19.95

MUSIC OF THE SPHERES, with Randy Masters. Randy Masters, a musician, composer and recording artist, has delved deeply into the study of sacred geometry, harmony and resonance, searching for the true knowledge of the music of the spheres. He has been a musician and educator about the science of music for many years. He has a unique understanding of the harmonic mathematics, and teaches about the ancient knowledge of Pythagoras and esoteric teachings. Randy Masters is a composer, publisher and multi-talented musician specializing in world music composition and performance. He also taught seven years at San Jose State University. He has released numerous recordings of multi-national jazz music and composed several feature-length movie scores. He specializes in spiritual teaching and harmonic attunements using special tuning forks designed from his research, color and essential oils. Randy explains how sound could be the key to unlocking and opening monuments such as the Hall of Records under the Sphinx, which contain information about advanced civilizations before Egypt. Randy also reveals how our bodies contain the microcosm of these codes that can be ignited through sound to explore these ancient structures. BACN-06a • 77 min Audio Tape • $12.00 / BACN-06 • 77 min VHS Video Tape • $19.95

TECHNOLOGY OF THE GODS, with David Hatcher Childress.
David Hatcher Childress is a real-life Indiana Jones. He has written a series of books about his journeys and research into lost cities and ancient mysteries of Africa, Arabia, China, Central Asia, India, South America Ancient Lemuria, Central America, Atlantis, Europe, as well as other locations. He is recognized as an expert not only on ancient civilizations and technology, but also on free energy, anti-gravity and UFOs. His books on these subjects include The Anti-Gravity Handbook, Extraterrestrial Archeology, The Free-Energy Device Handbook, and The Time Travel Handbook. In his lecture, he presents fascinating information on the advanced technology and anomalous architecture of our predecessors from around the globe. David Hatcher Childress provides a qualified presentation about his search for Atlantis, megalithic cultures and ancient technology. From the Hittite empire of the Middle East to the mountains of South America and the plains of Central America, records of ancient civilizations of an advanced nature are found throughout the world. In this presentation, Childress explores the massive cities high in the Andes and their links to Atlantis and Mu. A full two hours with over 200 slides from his travels around the world. Visit www.wexclub.com for more info. BACN-07a • 122 min Audio Tape • $12.00 / BACN-07 • 122 min VHS Video Tape • $19.95

ANCIENT WISDOM / NEW SCIENCE: 2000 Conference - Berkeley, California. Complete conference set. BACN-90a • 10+ hours on 7 audio tapes • $55.00 / BACN-90 • 10+ hours on 7 videotapes • $110.00

Ancient Wisdom / New Science - 2001 Conference

BIGFOOT / UFO CONNECTION, with Jack "Kewaunee" Lapseritis.. Kewaunee Lapseritis is a social scientist, applied anthropologist and health care professional who has thoroughly researched the Bigfoot/Sasquatch phenomenon for the last 45 years. In 1979, Kewaunee received the shock of his life when both a Bigfoot and ET simultaneously communicated with him telepathically. Since that time, he has documented 95 percipients, including a college professor, a government administrator and a whole array of people who have had similar psychic close encounters. Unlike many researchers looking for hard evidence of this elusive creature, Lapseritis has concentrated more on documenting the "experience" of the phenomenon, and gathering first-hand accounts of contacts. His "proof" is not a dead body, nor even a plaster cast, but takes the form of a consensus reality. That is, after hearing dozens of accounts of Sasquatch contact from witnesses who tell similar stories it is impossible for him not to accept the truth of these experiences. His findings are chronicled in his book, The Psychic Sasquatch and Their UFO Connection. BACN-08a • 102 min Audio Tape • $12.00 / BACN-08 • 102 min VHS Video Tape • $19.95

OUT-OF-BODY ADVENTURES, with Albert Taylor. Al Taylor, Ph.D., left behind nearly two decades of work as an aeronautical engineer/scientist to become a metaphysical researcher, teacher, lecturer and artist. Taylor describes his Out-of-Body (OBEs) with great insight and humor. Taylor reveals how these paranormal events have impacted his personal growth and relationships. Born and raised in Southern California, at seventeen, he elected to serve his country by enlisting into the United States Air Force. During his tour of duty in the USAF, he continued his education by attending nearby colleges and universities. His aerospace career continued as he performed development engineering on a top-secret program which has since become known as the F-117A Stealth Fighter. He was also involved in NASA's International Space Station program. After a myriad of paranormal events, and as a result of a spiritual awakening, Taylor left behind nearly two decades of work as an aeronautical engineer/scientist, to author and publish his book, Soul Traveler. With his characteristic wit, he reveals how paranormal events have impacted his personal growth and explain step-by-step how you can also have an OBE. BACN-09a • 93 min Audio Tape • $12.00 / BACN-09 • 93 min VHS Video Tape • $19.95

EGYPTIAN MYSTERIES, with Karena Bryan. Karena Bryan is a dynamic healer, writer, teacher and practitioner of the matriarchal Egyptian mysteries. She is a lifelong student of ancient and modern spiritual practice, with particular emphasis on social, cultural, and political anthropology as it applies to the Divine Feminine. As part of her ageless soul's quest for knowledge, particularly that knowledge which might be shared and utilized for the peaceful benefit of humankind and Mother Earth, Karena continues to study and practice numerous global traditions. This tape describes her travels and experience in and with the people of Egypt, and how their ancient mysteries touch even our modern society. Splitting her residence between the U.S. and Egypt, she has worked together with soul partner Hakim and co-authored a soon-to-be-published book: Egypt and The Awakening. Karena's training includes over ten years of study and practice of shamanic healing. In her presentation she provides a visual map of the role of the goddess and the sacred teachings of procreative alchemy. BACN-10a • 61 min Audio Tape • $12.00 / BACN-10 • 61 min VHS Video Tape • $19.95

UFOS AND RELIGION PANEL, with Stella Harder-Kucera, Moderator and Ted Peters. Jose Tirado and Matthew Fox, Panelists. Stella Harder-Kucera is a Filipina journalist, independent filmmaker and spiritual director who took a special reading course on UFOs with Dr. Ted Peters while pursuing the Master of Divinity/Master of Arts degree. Matthew Fox is a creation spirituality theologian who has been an ordained priest since 1967. A liberation theologian and progressive visionary, he was silenced by the Vatican and later dismissed from the Dominican order. He offers his insights on the phenomenon of UFOs, and how spirituality can be helpful in handling unexplained and unexpected experiences. Ted Peters is Professor of Systematic Theology at Pacific Lutheran Theological Seminary, Graduate Theological Union (GTU) in Berkeley, CA. He directs the Science and Religion Course Program at the Center for Theology and the Natural Sciences at the Graduate Theological Union. He has a longstanding theological interest in the possibility of extraterrestrial life in the universe. He is a Theology consultant for MUFON and was a former Louisiana MUFON Regional Director for Investigations. Jose Tirado is a Chaplain and Clinical Pastoral Education Supervisory Candidate at California Pacific Medical Center's Institute for Health and Healing. José is ordained as a Pastoral Care Minister in the Nalandabodhi Buddhist Community. BACN-11a • 86 min Audio Tape • $12.00 / BACN-11 • 86 min VHS Video Tape • $19.95

PARADIGM POLITICS, with Daniel Sheehan. Daniel Sheehan is a social activist who has spent virtually his entire life working on progressive social programs and initiatives. As the Legal Counsel on such nationally-recognized investigative cases involving government as The Karen Silkwood Case, The Iran/Contra Case, The Pentagon Papers Case, The Watergate Burglary Case, and The American Sanctuary Movement Case, Dan brings to the issue of Extraterrestrial Intelligence and the UFO Phenomenon a unique background in investigating and exposing the world of American governmental covert operations, "black budget" operations, mind control programs, government disinformation projects, covert warfare and clandestine operations. He established the Christic Institute in Washington, DC, which for nearly two decades was the country's preeminent public-interest law firm. Mr. Sheehan served as Legal Counsel for Dr. John Mack when he was called before a Harvard University faculty committee to answer for his position on alien abduction. Recently Daniel served as Director of "The Strategic Initiative to Identify the New Paradigm" for the State of the World Forum. He currently teaches World Politics at UC Santa Cruz and acts as General Counsel to Dr. Stephen Greer's Disclosure Project. BACN-12a • 115 min Audio Tape • $12.00 / BACN-12 • 115 min VHS Video Tape • $19.95

INTUITIVE ANIMAL COMMUNICATION, with Raphaela Pope. Raphaela Pope was a critical care nurse for many years before becoming a telepathic animal communicator. She has made her living for many years by talking to animals about life and death, about health and behavior problems, asking their opinions and discovering their desires. She has spoken with animals in their homes, shelters, rehabilitation centers, humane societies, on ranches, and in the wild. From this background of daily conversation and interaction, she has developed an authoritative vision about who and what animals are, what motivates them, and what their wisdom and insight can offer humans in an electronic age. She is an expert teacher, workshop leader, and sought-after speaker by animal clubs and organizations. Her journey is described in her book, Wisdom of Animals: Communication Between Animals and the People Who Love Them, which she co-wrote with Elizabeth Morrison. She helps people locate lost pets, solve behavior problems, diagnose illnesses and even simply find out what their pets are thinking. In her presentation she shares some simple techniques with the audience. BACN-13a • 79 min Audio Tape • $12.00 / BACN-13 • 79 min VHS Video Tape • $19.95

FORBIDDEN ARCHAEOLOGY, with Michael Cremo. Michael Cremo is on the cutting edge of science and culture issues. In the course of a few months' time he might be found on pilgrimage to sacred sites in India, appearing on a national television show, lecturing at a mainstream science conference, or speaking to an alternative science gathering. As he crosses disciplinary and cultural boundaries, he presents to his various audiences a compelling case for negotiating a new consensus on the nature of reality. Michael Cremo is a member of the History of Science Society, the World Archeological Congress, the Philosophy of Science Association, the European Association of Archaeologists and associate member of the Bhaktivedanta Institute specializing in history and philosophy of science. Michael Cremo's book Forbidden Archeology has become a classic in the history of archeology. It is filled with evidence showing that humans like us have existed on earth for tens of millions of years. This stands in stark contrast to the conventional scientific beliefs that humans like us have been present on this planet for only about 100,000 years. In his talk, Michael shows some of the more spectacular examples of what have been called out-of-place artifacts and outlines the extreme antiquity of humanity. He also explains how he was inspired by the ancient Sanskrit writings of India and other wisdom traditions. BACN-14a • 119 min Audio Tape • $12.00 / BACN-14 • 119 min VHS Video Tape • $19.95

ANCIENT WISDOM / NEW SCIENCE: 2001 Conference - Berkeley, California. Complete conference set. BACN-91a • 11 hours on 7 audio tapes • $55.00 / BACN-91 • 10 hours on 7 videotapes • $110.00

Ancient Wisdom / New Science - 2002 Conference

TALKING TO THE OTHER SIDE, with Mark Macy. Based in Boulder, Colorado, Macy is part of a growing international community of people working to contact the deceased. Mark Macy was an agnostic until a brush with colon cancer set him on a spiritual search in the 1980s. Then he learned about the miracles of Instrumental Trans-Communication (ITC): personal letters planted mysteriously in computers by invisible hands, images from other realms flashing across TV screens, and actual phone calls from angels. He immersed himself in ITC, and the amazing results of his research can be seen on his website www.worldITC.org and in his new book, 'Miracles in the Storm.' Imagine picking up the telephone one day and hearing the voice of a professional colleague – long deceased. These researchers use contemporary electronic technology – from audio and video recorders to personal computers – for documenting what they claim are communications from their friends and associates on "the other side." According to Macy, he and his earthside colleagues are joined in this bridge-building effort by a distinguished team of deceased scientists and artists who call themselves "Timestream." His mission is simple: to present graphic evidence that the worlds of the dead and the living are coming closer together. BACN-15a • 86 min Audio Tape • $12.00 / BACN-15 • 86 min VHS Video Tape • $19.95

NEW PARADIGMS FOR LOVE, with Deborah Taj Anapol. Deborah Taj Anapol attended Barnard College, graduated Phi Beta Kappa from UC Berkeley and received her Ph.D. in Clinical Psychology from the University of Washington in 1981. She is the author of Polyamory: The New Love Without Limits (1997), co-founder of Loving More magazine and producer of the Pelvic-Heart Integration videos (2002). Compersion: Using Jealousy as a Path to Unconditional Love is now available in Xerox pamphlet form, and she is currently at work on a book about balancing feminine and masculine energies. She currently works with individuals, couples and moresomes who are exploring New Paradigm relating and leads workshops nationwide on tantra, sexual healing, and polyamory with her tantric lover, Victor Gold. BACN-16a • 74 min Audio Tape • $12.00 / BACN-16 • 74 min VHS Video Tape • $19.95

NEWS MEDIA DECEPTIONS AND Cover-ups, with Terry Hansen. Terry Hansen is an independent journalist with an interest in scientific controversies and the politics of mass media. He is author of The Missing Times: News Media Complicity in the UFO Cover-up. He has organized and moderated two symposiums about the science and politics of UFO research for the Science Museum of Minnesota. Hansen holds a bachelor's degree in biology and a master's degree in science journalism, both from the University of Minnesota. He was a founding partner of KFH Publications, Inc., a Seattle computer-magazine publishing company. He is also an active private pilot with ratings for single-engine aircraft and gliders. This presentation covers some of the more recent and important stories that have been suppressed by the media cartels and powers-that-be. BACN-17a • 81 min Audio Tape • $12.00 / BACN-17 • 81 min VHS Video Tape • $19.95

MEDIA PANEL ON UFO'S: Lucia August. Moderator; Ralph Steiner, Leslie Kean, and Terry Hansen as Panelists. Lucia August is a Licensed Marriage and Family Therapist and Certified Hypnotherapist with a diverse private practice in Fremont, CA. She is the coordinator of the East Bay Contact Support Network and serves on the Board of Directors of the Bay Area Consciousness Network. Ralph Steiner is an independent producer and science journalist affiliated with KPFA and the Pacifica Radio Network. He brings to the UFO issue a knowledge of physics, molecular biology, genetics, astrophysics and information science. Leslie Kean is an investigative reporter, author and producer for Pacifica Radio. In May 2000, she published an investigative feature for the Boston Globe about the French report by high level military and space officials called "UFOs and Defense: What are we Prepared for?". In 2001, her story in the Providence Journal about pilot sightings of UFOs and possible aviation safety concerns was widely syndicated. Terry Hansen is an independent journalist with an interest in scientific controversies and the politics of mass media. He is author of The Missing Times: News Media Complicity in the UFO Cover-up. He has organized and moderated two symposia about the science and politics of UFO research for the Science Museum of Minnesota. Hansen holds a bachelor's degree in biology and a master's degree in science journalism, both from the University of Minnesota. BACN-18a • 68 min Audio Tape • $12.00 / BACN-18 • 68 min VHS Video Tape • $19.95

THE TRUTH ABOUT 9-11, with Carol Brouillet. Carol Brouillet is a Co-Founder of the International Media Project, which produces Making Contact, a half-hour radio program now heard on over 165 stations, primarily in the U.S. and Canada. (Making Contact will also pilot a new daily show beginning in February 2001.) Carol also helped found the Who's Counting Project, which promotes the film Who's Counting? Marilyn Waring on Sex, Lies & Global Economics. Both non-profits seek to connect people, vital ideas and important information to nurture healthy social change, economic justice and ecological sustainability. A passionate advocate of local currencies to raise consciousness, nurture community, and increase local self-reliance, her paper Reinventing Money, Restoring the Earth, Reweaving the Web of Life has won an honourable mention from the Millennium Institute as one of the best ideas for the 21st Century. BACN-19a • 91 min Audio Tape • $12.00 / BACN-19 • 91 min VHS Video Tape • $19.95

ANCIENT EGYPTIAN HI-TECH, with Christopher Dunn. Christopher Dunn has an extensive background as a master craftsman, starting as a journeyman lathe turner in his hometown of Manchester, England. Recruited by an American aerospace company, he immigrated to the United States in 1969. The author's pyramid odyssey began in 1977 when he read Peter Tompkins' book Secrets of the Great Pyramid. His immediate reaction to the Giza Pyramid's schematics was that this edifice was a gigantic machine. Discovering the purpose of this machine and documenting his case has taken the better part of twenty years of research. In the process he has published a dozen magazine articles, including the much-quoted "Advanced Machining in Ancient Egypt" in Analog, and has had his research referenced in such books as Graham Hancock's "Fingerprints of the Gods" and Cohn Wilson's "From Atlantis to the Sphinx". Chris Dunn, his wife Jeanne and their children live in Danville, Illinois. In 1998, he published the groundbreaking book The Giza Power Plant: Technologies of Ancient Egypt, which proposed that the Great Pyramid of Giza was actually a large acoustical device that produced energy. BACN-20a • 113 min Audio Tape • $12.00 / BACN-20 • 113 min VHS Video Tape • $19.95

NEW SCIENCE BREAKTHROUGHS, with Joe Firmage. Joe Firmage founded his first company, Serius, at age 18, embarking on a career in science and technology research, which has included everything from Internet consulting to investigating JFK's UFO intelligence files. Currently chairman of Motion Sciences Organization, he will explain how physics can advance technologies for nonpolluting energy generation and land, sea, air and space transportation systems. Includes a question and answer session that discusses some of the new technology that is in development by various companies and individuals. BACN-21a • 70 min Audio Tape • $12.00 / BACN-21 • 70 min VHS Video Tape • $19.95

ANCIENT WISDOM / NEW SCIENCE: 2002 Conference – Berkeley, California. Complete conference set. BACN-92a • 10 hours on 7 audio tapes • $55.00 / BACN-92 • 10 hours on 7 videotapes • $110.00

The Aztec UFO 2002 Symposium

THE INTERCEPTION: ROSWELL CRASH SITE METAL RECOVERY, with Dennis Balthaser. Dennis Balthaser, concentrates his research on the 1947 Roswell Incident, Area 51 and Underground Bases. In this presentation he talked about his Interception experience. While still affiliated with the International UFO Museum in Roswell, NM, in 1997 as the UFO investigator, he was contacted by a gentleman in Oklahoma claiming his father had been a military policeman at the Roswell crash site and had a piece of the metal from the crashed vehicle. Balthaser made arrangements to travel to Oklahoma to meet the gentleman and obtain the metal for testing, but was never able to meet with them. Instead he was met and intercepted by people claiming to be United States Air Force, Office of Special Investigation agents. In this lecture Balthaser gives a detailed account of the events that transpired from the original phone

call through the current investigation, which is still on-going. Balthaser was in the United States Army in an Engineering Battalion. He moved to Roswell, NM in 1996, to pursue his 25 year interest in UFOlogy and particularly the Roswell Incident, Underground Bases and Area 51. Aztec-01a • 2 Hour Audio Tape • $12.00 / Aztec-01 • 2 Hour VHS Video Tape • $19.95

MYSTERIOUS UFO INCIDENT IN PENNSYLVANIA AND BIG FOOT, with Stan Gordon. This presentation includes a detailed account of the 1965 UFO crash incident near Kecksburg, PA, and the bizarre 1973 UFO/Bigfoot outbreak in the state. Stan Gordon's UFO/Phenomena Biographical Information: Born October 30, 1949 in Pittsburgh, Stan was trained as an electronics technician who has specialized in the area of radio communications. He is presently active in the advanced consumer electronics sales field. Stan's interest in UFO's and other unusual happenings began at age 10. Since 1965, Stan has been conducting investigations into thousands of UFO and other strange encounters reported across Pennsylvania. During the late 1960's, Stan acted as a telephone report sighting coordinator for the UFO Research Institute of Pittsburgh. Stan has been internationally recognized as an authority on the subject of the UFO and Bigfoot phenomena. He gained prominence from his firsthand investigation into the well-remembered 1973 Bigfoot/ UFO series of sightings and encounters which occurred in Pennsylvania. This outbreak brought worldwide attention to the subject, and was a major news story in the media for several weeks. Due to copyright restrictions this tape does not include the slides. Aztec-02a • 2 Hour Audio Tape • $12.00 / Aztec-02 • 2 Hour VHS Video Tape • $19.95

UFOS: THE TECHNOLOGY ISSUE, with John Schuessler. John Schuessler is a founding member of the Mutual UFO Network, Inc., and is currently the MUFON International Director and a member of the Board of Directors. As a staff member he has written numerous articles for SKYLOOK and the MUFON UFO Journal and has been a featured speaker as many MUFON symposia. He is a member of the UFO Research Coalition Board of Directors and a member of the Science Advisory Board for the National Institute for Discovery Science. He first became active in UFO research in 1965 when he joined the Aerial Phenomena Research Organization. John is an aerospace consultant specializing in space commercialization and space tourism. Prior to his retirement from Boeing he was involved engineering for most human space flight programs including Gemini, Skylab, Space Shuttle and the International Space Station. On his last major project, he was Program Manager for the design and construction of the new NASA Neutral Buoyancy Laboratory and in 1997, he received the NASA Public Service Medal for his leadership on the project. Aztec-03a • 2 Hour Audio Tape • $12.00 / Aztec-03 • 2 Hour VHS Video Tape • $19.95

THE DAY AFTER ROSWELL: REVELATIONS FROM BEYOND THE GRAVE, with Karl Pflock. Karl Pflock, author, consultant, and UFO researcher, is the author of numerous works of fiction and nonfiction. He has written and ghostwritten several nonfiction books and has been a consulting senior editor for Arlington House Publishers, editor of Libertarian Review, a senior editor at the American Enterprise Institute, contributing editor to Reason, and science columnist for Eternity Science Fiction. His articles on UFOs have appeared in such journals as Fortean Times, Omni, the International UFO Reporter, The Anomalist, Fate, the MUFON UFO Journal, Cuadernos de Ufología (Spain), and the MUFON 1995 International UFO Symposium Proceedings, and he has made significant contributions to other U.S. and foreign publications. A popular speaker at UFO and anomalous phenomena gatherings, he was named 1998 UFOlogist of the Year by the National UFO Conference. Mr. Pflock's interest in UFOs is virtually lifelong, and his investigations have left no doubt in his mind that UFOs are real. In the late 1960s and early 1970s he served as a member and chairman of the National Capital Area [investigations] Subcommittee of the National Investigations Committee on Aerial Phenomena (NICAP), then the world's largest private UFO research organization. Aztec-04a • 106 min Audio Tape • $12.00 / Aztec-04 • 106 min VHS Video Tape • $19.95

CRITIQUE OF THE ROSWELL CRITICS, with Stanton Friedman. Stanton T. Friedman was born in New Jersey on July 29, 1934. He was named valedictorian of his 1951 Linden, New Jersey, high school class and spent two years at Rutgers University in New Brunswick, New Jersey before switching to the University of Chicago in 1953. He received BS and MS degrees in Physics from UC in 1955 and 1956, where Carl Sagan was a classmate. He worked for fourteen years as a nuclear physicist for such companies as General Electric, General Motors, Westinghouse, TRW, Aerojet General Nucleonics, and McDonnell Douglas on such advanced, highly classified, eventually canceled projects as nuclear aircraft, fission and fusion rockets, and nuclear power plants for space. Since 1967 he has lectured on the topic Flying Saucers Are Real at more than 600 colleges and over 100 professional groups in fifty states, nine Canadian provinces, England, Italy, Germany, Holland, France, Finland, Brazil, Australia, Korea, Mexico, Turkey, Argentina, and Israel. He has published more than 70 papers on UFOs besides his dozens of conventional articles and appeared on hundreds of radio and TV shows. Stan is the original civilian investigator of the Roswell Incident, who co-authored Crash at Corona and instigated the Unsolved Mysteries Roswell program. Aztec-05a • 2 Hour Audio Tape • $12.00 / Aztec-05 • 2 Hour VHS Video Tape • $19.95

AZTEC 1949-1950: NEW INFORMATION ON THE AZTEC UFO CRASH, with Linda Moulton Howe. Linda Moulton Howe, Emmy Award-winning TV producer, investigative reporter and writer, will present eyewitness accounts and documents about a "dog fight" of silver discs in the sky over Aztec followed by a crash and retrieval of one disc from Hart Canyon in March 1949; multiple disc flyovers by the hundreds the next year on March 17, 1950 reported in The Denver Post and The Farmington Daily Times; and alleged government knowledge and cover-up of the Aztec disc crash and subsequent disc flyovers. Linda Moulton Howe is a graduate of Stanford University with a Masters Degree in Communication. She has devoted her documentary film, television and radio career to productions concerning science, medicine and the environment. Ms. Howe has received local, national and international awards, including three regional Emmys and a national Emmy nomination. Those films have included Poison in the Wind and A Sun Kissed Poison which compared smog pollution in Los Angeles and Denver; Fire In The Water about hydrogen as an alternative energy source to fossil fuels; A Radioactive Water about uranium contamination of public drinking water in a Denver suburb; and A Strange Harvest which explored the worldwide animal mutilation mystery that has haunted the United States and other countries since the late 1950s and continues to date. Aztec-06a • 2 Hour Audio Tape • $12.00 / Aztec-06 • 2 Hour VHS Video Tape • $19.95

HOW THE WAR ON TERROR INTERRUPTED ET CONTACT, with Jim Marrs. A native of Fort Worth, Texas, Mr. Marrs earned a Bachelor of Arts degree in journalism from the University of North Texas in 1966 and attended Graduate School at Texas Tech in Lubbock for two years more. He has worked for several Texas newspapers, including the Fort Worth Star-Telegram, where beginning in 1968 he served as police reporter. Mr. Marrs then became a general-assignments reporter covering stories locally, in Europe and the Middle East. After a leave of absence to serve with a Fourth Army intelligence unit during the Vietnam War, he became military and aerospace writer for the newspaper and an investigative reporter. Since 1980, Mr. Marrs has been a freelance writer and public relations consultant. Since 1976, Mr. Marrs has taught a course on the assassination of President John F. Kennedy at the University of Texas at Arlington. In 1989, his book, Crossfire: The Plot That Killed Kennedy, was published to critical acclaim and within three years had gone into an eighth printing in both hardbound and softbound editions. Crossfire reached the New York Times Paperback Non-Fiction Best Seller list in mid-February 1992 and remained there for more than six weeks. His book became a basis for the Oliver Stone film JFK. Mr. Marrs served as a chief consultant for both the films screenplay and production. Mr. Marrs has appeared on ABC, NBC, CBS, CNN, CSPAN, the Discovery, Learning and History Channels, This Morning America, Geraldo, Montell Williams, Today and The Larry King and Art Bell radio programs. Aztec-07a • 2 Hour Audio Tape • $12.00 / Aztec-07 • 2 Hour VHS Video Tape • $19.95

AZTEC UFO SYMPOSIUM: 2002 Conference - Aztec, New Mexico. Complete conference set. AZTEC-92a • 14 hours on 7 audio tapes • $55.00 / AZTEC-92 • 14 hours on 7 videotapes • $110.00

The Aztec UFO 2003 Symposium

UFO INCIDENTS IN ENGLAND, with Nick Redfern. Nick Redfern. Aztec-08a • 2 Hour Audio Tape • $12.00 / Aztec-08 • 2 Hour VHS Video Tape • $19.95

ATTACKED BY A FLYING SAUCER, with Karl Pflock. Karl Pflock. Aztec-09a • 2 Hour Audio Tape • $12.00 / Aztec-09 • 2 Hour VHS Video Tape • $19.95

INSIDE OF THE BALCK VAULT, with John Greenewald, Jr. John Greenewald, Jr. Aztec-10a • 2 Hour Audio Tape • $12.00 / Aztec-10 • 2 Hour VHS Video Tape • $19.95

CRITIQUING THE MAJESTIC 12 CRITICS, with Stanton Friedman. John Greenewald, Jr. Aztec-11a • 2 Hour Audio Tape • $12.00 / Aztec-11 • 2 Hour VHS Video Tape • $19.95

THE UFO PhENOMENON: 56 Years and Still a Mystery, with Robert Swiatek. Robert Swiatek. Aztec-12a • 106 min Audio Tape • $12.00 / Aztec-12 • 106 min VHS Video Tape • $19.95

THE FRANK SCULLY TAPES, with Wendy Connors. Wendy Connors. Aztec-13a • 2 Hour Audio Tape • $12.00 / Aztec-13• 2 Hour VHS Video Tape • $19.95

UFOS AND MACHINE INTELLIGENCE: Looking at the Pros and Cons, with Richard Dolan. Richar Dolan. Aztec-14a • 2 Hour Audio Tape • $12.00 / Aztec-14 • 2 Hour VHS Video Tape • $19.95

SCIENTIFIC RESEARCH OF THE UFO PHENOMENON, with Bruce Maccabee. Bruce Maccabee. Aztec-15a • 2 Hour Audio Tape • $12.00 / Aztec-15 • 2 Hour VHS Video Tape • $19.95

AZTEC UFO SYMPOSIUM: 2002 Conference - Aztec, New Mexico. Complete conference set. AZTEC-93a • 14 hours on 7 audio tapes • $55.00 / AZTEC-93 • 14 hours on 7 videotapes • $110.00

MUFON International UFO Symposium 2002

UFOS AND REALITY TRANSFORMATION, with Chris Styles. Chris Styles is a Canadian UFO researcher who has been an active investigator of both classic and current UFO cases that have occurred along the Atlantic Ocean in Canada. His work on the Shag Harbour Incident has had tremendous impact on the way that UFO crash / retrieval scenarios are viewed. In 1994, Chris received a grant from the Fund for UFO Research to help underwrite the cost of an extensive document search that involved non-transferable Canadian military documents held at Canada's National Archives in Ottawa. Some of the results of that search are included in this presentation. He has written custom software used in both printing and UFOlogy which automates many of the measurements needed in tedious video analysis. And in 1995, Chris directed an underwater search for physical evidence that might have remained submerged and undetected below the surface of Shag Harbour. Paramount Television financed the expedition that employed divers, sidescan sonar, underwater video and magnetometers in their search to uncover evidence from this fascinating incident. MUFON-01a • 76 min Audio • $12.00 / MUFON-01 • 76 min Video • $19.95

THE DAY AFTER PHIL CORSO, with William J. Birnes. Dr. William J. Birnes is a New York Times best selling author with Col. Philip Corso for The Day After Roswell. Dr. Birnes is also a new York literary publishing agent and an editor at McGraw-Hill. Birnes is also the publisher of UFO Magazine in Los Angeles and the Editor-in-Chief of the UFO Encyclopedia at Pocket Books, a division of Simon & Schuster in New York. He is a New Jersey native who currently resides in southern California. A true-crime writer who books have become required reading at Harvard Law School, Birnes has recently completed a psychology textbook for

police and homicide investigators. In this lecture, Birnes describes his involvement with helping Lt. Col. Philip J. Corso in the publication of his book "The Day After Roswell." MUFON-02a • 82 min Audio • $12.00 / MUFON-02 • 82 min Video • $19.95

SCIENTIFIC CONNECTIONS IN PHOTO/VIDEO UFOLOGY, with Jeff Sainio. Graduating Magna Cum Laude from Northern Michigan University with a BS in Math-Computer Science in 1979, Jeff W. Sainio made a career switch from the broadcast engineering field to managing a major printing firm in Wisconsin. His work has netted seven US patents in the imaging and aerodynamics fields. Being an F.C.C. licensed broadcast engineer, his knowledge is useful in video analysis at the electronic as well as imaging level. Jeff's interest in UFOs was piqued during the 1965 flap when two discs were sighted by respected policemen in his hometown in northern Michigan. He joined MUFON in February 1991 and is the Staff Photoanalyst for still photographs and videotapes. He has been performing computer enhancement and analysis of UFO photographs and videotapes submitted to him by either MUFON or directly from the photographers. Mr. Sainio is recognized worldwide for his expertise in this field and has appeared on numerous national television show demonstrating techniques for determining the authenticity of UFO photographs and videos. In this presentation he outlines these techniques and describes working with some of more popular and recent footage of UFOs. MUFON-03a • 68 min Audio • $12.00 / MUFON-03 • 68 min Video • $19.95

THE LIMITS OF SCIENCE IN UFO RESEARCH, with Richard Dolan. Richard Dolan is the author of "UFOs and the National Security State," published by Keyhole Publishing, which covers the period from 1941 to 1973 and provides a thorough historical analysis of the national security dimensions of the UFO phenomenon. Born in Brooklyn and raised on Long Island, Dolan earned a scholarship to study at Oxford University, where he closely missed receiving a Rhodes Scholarship. After completing his graduate work at the University of Rochester he became a self-employed business writer to earn a living. Around 1994 he began to develop and interest in the UFO problem. He approached UFOs by looking at the history and politics of the phenomenon. He was intrigued by the cultural schizophrenia involved in the subject and with the fact that mainstream and academic culture continued to treat UFOs as amusement, but that some many intelligent people take it seriously. In this presentation he discusses using science and peer review to examine UFOs and national security. MUFON-04a • 70 min Audio • $12.00 / MUFON-04 • 70 min Video • $19.95

IN SEARCH OF EBE'S, with William Hamilton. Bill read the book "Flying Saucers from Outer Space" by Donald Keyhoe when still in grade school. By the time he went to high school, he was actively pursuing interests in the UFO phenomenon. He met and became acquainted with the early UFO contactees by attending the Giant Rock spacecraft conventions hosted by George Van Tassel. Hamilton has had over one hundred personal sightings of UFOs. In 1976, he investigated his first UFO abduction case and applied for membership in MUFON as a field investigator. He is currently Executive Director of Skywatch International, founded by Col. Steve Wilson. In this lecture he presents how new findings in planetary science and new discoveries and theories in biology have a bearing on UFO studies. He also discusses the new perspectives offered by these conclusions and their relevance toward resolving the mystery of UFO origins. MUFON-05a • 75 min Audio • $12.00 / MUFON-05 • 75 min Video • $19.95

FIVE THEMES ON UFO ABDUCTION, with Dan Wright. Dan Wright has a masters degree in political affairs from the University of Illinois, Springfield. He joined MUFON in 1978, where his positions included state section director, state director for Michigan, central states regional director, and deputy director for investigations. Dan was on the MUFON board for 15 years, seven as deputy director. His accomplishments at MUFON over the years include the revised computer input database and initial computer catalog of MUFON case files; writing several chapters in the field investigator's manual on proper interviewing techniques and on completing the general cases and computer input forms; distribution of a photo slide set for MUFON presentations; and initiation of a regular newsletter to and annual meeting for all state directors. From 1992 until 1997, he directed the abduction transcription project for MUFON. Twenty abduction researchers contributed 930 audio cassette tapes of hypnosis sessions and interviews with 265 suspected abductees. In this presentation he details the five themes found in many abduction cases, as based on a key-word index containing nearly 2,500 entries from transcripts of those sessions. MUFON-06a • 73 min Audio • $12.00 / MUFON-06 • 73 min Video • $19.95

BUILDING A PROFESSIONAL COMMUNITY, with David Jacobs. Dr. David M. Jacobs is Associate Professor of History at Temple University specializing in twentieth century American history and culture. His is former Director of the American Studies Program. Dr. Jacobs has been a UFO researcher for 35 year. In 1973, he completed his doctoral dissertation in the field of intellectual history at the University of Wisconsin - Madison on the controversy over unidentified flying objects in America. This was only the second Ph.D. degree granted involving a UFO-related theme. Indiana University Press published a revised version of his dissertation as "The UFO Controversy in America" in 1975. It was the first positive book towards UFOs published by an academic press. In this lecture he discusses how both the UFO phenomenon and the UFO research community have presented almost insurmountable barriers to scientific engagement with the data. MUFON-07a • 73 min Audio • $12.00 / MUFON-07 • 73 min Video • $19.95

CONFLICTING INTEREST IN THE CONTROL OF EXTRATERRESTRIAL INTELLIGENCE, with Timothy Good. Timothy Good became interested in UFOs in 1955 when he read a book by Donald Keyhoe describing sightings by qualified observers such as military and civilian pilots. He has become a leading authority on the subject, researching sightings worldwide, amassing a wealth of evidence, including thousands of intelligence documents. His numerous contacts include astronauts, military and intelligence chiefs, pilots and politicians. In 1987, Good published "Above Top Secret" which became an instant bestseller and is regarded by many as the definitive book on the subject, together with the fully updated book replacing it, "Beyond Top Secret" in 1996, which spent five weeks on the Sunday Times best-seller list. His latest book, "Unearthly Disclosure," published in 2000, was serialized in London's Daily Mail. Timothy is also a professional violinist, and played for fourteen years with the London Symphony Orchestra. He is without a doubt, one of the world's most respected authorities on the alien phenomenon. In this lecture he discloses extraordinary information provided to him via a high-ranking source that confirms that aliens have established subterranean and submarine bases on Earth and that contact has been made with a select group in the U.S. Military and scientific intelligence community. MUFON-08a • 77 min Audio • $12.00 / MUFON-08 • 77 min Video • $19.95

AIR TRAFFIC CONTROL ZONES, PILOTS, AIRCRAFT AND UFOS, with Don Ledger. Don ledger is a writer and the author of three books. His most recent book, "Dark Object," co-authored with Chris Styles, deals with the alleged UFO crash in Shag Harbour, Nova Scotia in October 1967. Mr. Ledger is a regular contributor to the Toronto-based radio show Strange Days Indeed, hosted by Errol Bruce-Knapp. He has been involved in half a dozen television documentaries dealing with both the Shag Harbour Incident and UFOs in general, as well as numerous radio shows in both Canada and the United States. He become and active investigator of the UFO phenomenon over ten years ago. In this lecture he discusses the misinterpretation of air regulations and air traffic control systems and regulations by UFO researchers, some scientists and the lay public when UFO incidents occur in regulated airspace or near aircraft. MUFON-09a • 78 min Audio • $12.00 / MUFON-09 • 78 min Video • $19.95

THE ABDUCTION PHENOMENON - WHERE WE ARE NOW? with Budd Hopkins. Budd Hopkins, a New York artist, is famous for his three important books: Missing Time (1981), Intruders (1987), and Witnessed (1996). On a summer afternoon in 1964, Budd Hopkins and two others watched a small, round metallic craft maneuver in the sky over Cape Cod. This daylight sighting marked the beginning of Hopkin's interest in the UFO phenomenon, but his first nationally known investigation didn't tale place until 1975. At that time, a UFO apparently landed in a New Jersey park only one mile from Manhattan and was seen by a number of witnesses. Mr Hopkin's carefully researched account of this landing and the observation of ten or eleven occupants, appeared in "The Village Voice," and "Cosmopolitan" magazine and elsewhere, and was covered extensively by television and radio. Throughout the years, his goal has been to bring an objective, dispassionate, scientific intelligence to bear on the UFO abduction phenomenon. In pursuit of this goal he founded, in 1989, "the Intruders Foundation," a not-for-profit organization devoted to research and public education concerning this extraordinary enigma. In this lecture he discusses several things that are known with assurance about the UFO phenomenon as well as some of the theories that can be confidently pronounced as incorrect. He covers some of the latest research, particularly in the area of abductions, and provides a summary where were are now with the abduction phenomenon. MUFON-10a • 72 min Audio • $12.00 / MUFON-10 • 72 min Video • $19.95

AN AMERICAN IN SUFFOLK: THE RENDLESHAM FOREST UFO INCIDENT, with Peter Robbins. Peter is currently the Editor-in-Chief of the website www.ufocity.com and writes a column for "UFO Magazine" called "Webwatch." Robbins has been involved with the UFO field for many years. In 1977 he created and produced "The Question of UFOs," a series of six half-hour programs for Channel C, Manhattan Cable TV. In 1992, Robbins was appointed Executive Assistant for the Intruders Foundation, based in New York City. In this lecture he discussed his reflections, observation and updates on a decade of research in Britain's Rendlesham Forest UFO incident. He also discusses his role in the publication of "Left at East Gate" with Larry Warren and talks about some afterthoughts on the books and the events which inspired it. He also reveals some of the situations and people who never made it into the book, and wither the book had any impact on official government policies pertaining to UFOs in the United Kingdom. MUFON-11a • 90 min Audio • $12.00 / MUFON-11 • 90 min Video • $19.95

MIRACLES: UFO CONTACT, with Betty Hill. Betty Hill is a life-long resident of New Hampshire. She graduated from the University of New Hampshire, with a BS Degree in Social Work and was employed by the State of New Hampshire as a social worker, until her retirement in 1975. Following her UFO sighting and abduction experience in 1961, Betty has spent many years doing television and radio programs, college lectue tours and writing assignments. She is the author of the book "A Common Sense Approach to UFOs." Betty is also the subject of John Fuller's book "Interrupted Journey," and the television movie "The UFO Incident." In this lecture she describes her (and her husband Barney's) abduction experience and provides some anecdotes and reflections on the 40 years that has passed since it occurred. At the end of the presentation she displays the blue dress she was wearing with the even happened back in 1961. MUFON-12a • 68 Min Audio • $12.00 / MUFON-12 • 68 Min Video • $19.95

ARE THERE UFOS ON MARS? with Richard Thieme. Richard Thieme speaks, writes and consults on the human dimensions of technology and work, including information security, organizational culture and the dynamics of leadership and communications. He is a regular featured speaker at the Black Hat Briefings and Def Con and a contributing editor for Information Security Magazine. Thieme's creative use of the Internet to reach global markets has earned accolades around the world. Thieme has published widely. Translated into German, Chinese, Japanese, Slovene, Danish and Indonesian, his articles are taught at numerous universities in Europe, Australia, Canada, and the United States. His is a contributing editor for Information Security Magazine and has written for Secure Business Quarterly, Forbes, Wires, Computer Underground Digest and Salon. His article "Stalking the UFO Mime on the Internet" is the basis of education at universities in Europe, Canada, Australia and the United States. His interest in UFOs began in the 1950s, when he had first heard of them as a child. In this lecture he discusses the evidence for the evidence of UFOs. He also talks about the consensus reality of the UFO phenomenon, from the religious metaphors to the views of the general public on UFOs. MUFON-13a • 49 min Audio • $12.00 / MUFON-13 • 49 min Video • $19.95

TURKISH UFO INVESTIGATION, with Esen Sekerkarar. Esen Sekerkarar is a young Turkish woman who is vice-president of a very active UFO association in Istanbul. She is an integral part of the annual Turkish UFO symposium, and has also helped to create a new UFO museum in Istanbul. In this lecture, Esen presents some interesting facts and observations about new UFO sightings in Turkey, including the recent video footage of a UFO shooting down an incoming meteor. MUFON-14a • 79 min Audio • $12.00 / MUFON-14 • 79 min Video • $19.95

MUFON FIELD INVESTIGATOR TRAINING, with Dan Wright. UFOlogy is the study of the UFO phenomenon. At its core is the investigation of UFO reports as made by human witnesses, the enigmatic source of the original sighting typically having long since departed. With close encounters and other so-called "high strangeness" cases, a thorough investigation is even more necessary, especially where episodes of "missing time" and other psychological or physiological effects are reported by the witness(es). This two-hour video presentation was recorded at a recent Field Investigator training class. Makes a great companion to the MUFON Field Investigator's Manual, now in a newly revised fourth edition. MUFON-15a • 115 min Audio • $12.00 / MUFON-15 • 115 min Video • $19.95

MUFON INTERNATIONAL UFO SYMPOSIUM: 2002 Conference - Rochester, New York. Complete conference set. MUFON-92a • 19 hours on 15 audio tapes • $110.00 / MUFON-92 • 19 hours on 15 videotapes • $220.00

MYSTERY OF AMERICA: VOLUME 1 – ENIGMATIC MYSTERIES AND ANOMALOUS ARTIFACTS OF NORTH AMERICA: A CONNECTION TO THE ANCIENT PAST, with Tédd St. Rain. Mysterious and often inexplicable remnants of civilization's history fascinate scientists and archaeologists. People travel worldwide to visit such sites, yet some of the most enigmatic artifacts and structures have been found right here in North America. Unfortunately, because these records do not fit within accepted academic models of human history, they remain unexplained mysteries, and most people never hear of them. Long before any humans were supposed to be on this continent, unknown hands removed millions of pounds of copper from mines near Lake Superior. Giant people as tall as 12 feet were buried in Arizona, Nevada and the Midwest. A three-foot-high adult mummy was discovered in Wyoming. A "hinged silver bell" with indecipherable writing was blasted from 15 feet below the ground in Massachusetts. A human-like tooth, three times normal size, was found in coal from a Montana mine. Sandaled feet made footprints in rock at least 300 million years old in Utah. According to modern wisdom, humans evolved on Earth no earlier than two million years ago. Yet many of these artifacts were made or recorded long before then. How can this be? Could any of these anomalies have been the result of an advanced civilization once present on our planet? This book presents the evidence that there have been intelligent beings on earth long before humans are thought to have evolved here. Explore these intriguing possibilities and more in this exciting and informative investigation into the mysteries and anomalous artifacts of North America. Tédd St. Rain, author, lecturer, and videographer, he has traveled the world extensively investigating the world's ancient mysteries and enigmas, actively researching the mysterious, the metaphysical and the mythical. Born in Long Beach, California, Tédd is the owner of Lost Arts Media that publishes, markets and distributes fascinating and educational books, videos and multimedia products to help inform, enlighten and inspire humanity. In this presentation Tédd has collected 80 of his best slides in an effort to explain the "most unusual of the unusual" found in the crypto-archaeological literature. Recorded at the International MUFON Symposium in Dearborn, MI, in July 2003 this tape reveals the mysteries that have occurred in our past. Coming soon on DVD, call for details. MUFON-17a • 60 min Audio • $12.00 / MUFON-17v • 60 min Video • $19.95

ANCIENT MYSTERIES OF NORTH AMERICA, by Tédd St. Rain. See page 88. AMNA-01a • 110 min Audio Tape • $12.00 / AMNA-01 • 110 min VHS Video Tape • $19.95

The New Living Expo 2003 (continued)

RELEASE THE WRITER WITHIN! with Thea Sullivan. End Creative Struggle and Find the Flow There's a reason you want to write - because something wants to be created through you! Learn how to drop judgment, doubt, and fear and become the writer you already are. Experience the sacred state of trust and deep listening, where ideas arrive effortlessly and writing becomes a transcendent experience of being in the flow. Sullivan is a published poet, renowned coach, and creator of the popular Intuitive Voice creative writing workshops. She helps people around the country free their unique writers' voices. NLE-13a • 45 min Audio • $12.00 / NLE-13v • 45 min Video • $19.95

DENTAL MERCURY, SILVER FILLING AND BODY ILLNESS, with Dr. James Rota. With growing scientific evidence regarding the effects of the mercury in our silver dental fillings, some countries have banned it while others are limiting its use. Legislation and lawsuits are being pursued. Dr. Rota, a UCLA educator and clinician for the past 40 years, will share his experience with this highly toxic substance and explore how to detoxify our body of mercury, the second most deadly metal on earth. Dr. Rota, a former UCLA professor and practicing dentist, has lectured around the world and appeared on television regarding his 30-year investigation of illnesses related to dental mercury filling. NLE-14a • 45 min Audio • $12.00 / NLE-14v • 45 min Video • $19.95

PRACTICAL APPLICATIONS OF LIGHT AND HEAT THERAPY, with Dave Olszewski. Find out how sunlight, artificial lighting and hyper-thermal- heat affect your health. David discusses the uses and benefits of sunlight, full-spectrum lighting, soft lasers, LED's, phototherapy and heat-therapy. Learn the real truth about ultraviolet light and how to counteract the negative effects of fluorescent lighting and computer screen radiation. Discover five methods to boost your immune systems and detoxify — naturally. Olszewski is an engineer, author, and lecturer; He is president of Light Energy Company and coauthor of Light Years Ahead. He holds the patent for Light Therapy Equipment. NLE-15a • 45 min Audio • $12.00 / NLE-15v • 45 min Video • $19.95

ALL ABOUT BLOOD SUGAR REGULATION, with Rick Dina. This interactive and informative presentation will clearly illustrate the vital importance of proper blood sugar and insulin regulation as it relates to many key aspects of health. Topics include diabetes, cardiovascular disease, wrinkles, aging and longevity. Participants will be empowered with the dietary and lifestyle tools necessary and learn to apply them to their lives for maximum benefit. Fundamental principles, up-todate research, and an informative note packet will be provided. A popular Bay Area lecturer, former staff doctor at True North Health Center and Naturopathic Medical School instructor, Dr. Dina specializes in nutrition/lifestyle consulting in his South Bay Chiropractic practice. NLE-16a • 45 min Audio • $12.00 / NLE-16v • 45 min Video • $19.95

OXYGEN - THE BREATH OF LIFE, with Sandy Harton. Oxygen therapies have proven to be effective against pathogens, bacteria, yeasts, molds, fungi, parasites, even cancer. These therapies will be discussed, focusing on the technology used in the product Hydroxygen Plus. Hydroxygen Plus is aerobic and pH enhancing. Pathogens and other invaders are anaerobic and thrive in acidic conditions. When you eliminate the cause of ill health (i.e. acid & pathogens, etc.), wellness returns. Harton is a Certified Nutritional Microscopist, and a national trainer and educator of nutrition and the proper use of health products. Ms. Harton provides training and development for other nutritionally minded consultants. NLE-17a • 45 min Audio • $12.00 / NLE-17v • 45 min Video • $19.95

HYPERBARIC OXYGEN THERAPY - THERAPY FOR THE NEW MILLENNIUM, with Todd S. Kaufmann. Hyperbaric oxygen therapy is the application of placing oxygen under pressure within an enclosed chamber to increase the amount of absorbable oxygen into the bloodstream. The increased pressure helps to force more oxygen-enriched blood deeper into the body tissues and organs. Hyperbaric oxygen therapy is quite successful in treating chronic or difficult health conditions such as: Chronic Fatigue Syndrome, Fibromyalgia, Headaches, Strokes, Nerve/Circulatory disorders, wound healing, and many other conditions. Kaufmann is both a practicing Chiropractor and Director of the Hyperbaric Therapy Center of Marin located in Corte Madera. NLE-18a • 45 min Audio • $12.00 / NLE-18v • 45 min Video • $19.95

LYMPH : HOW THE MIND AND SPIRIT AFFECT THE BODY, with Peggy Parker. In addition to learning how your lymphatic system works, you will explore the relationship between your immune system, diet, stress levels, and spiritual health as they relate to your lymphatic system. Anyone struggling with water retention, cellulite, fatigue, or any chronic degenerative illness can go away with practical information as well as learning tools to change their state of health today. Experts and novices will learn something here. Parker holds her Doctorate in Naturopathic and Integrative Biological Medicine and is the Medical Director and founder of Fusion MediSpa, a fully integrated health care facility located in Northern Idaho. NLE-19a • 45 min Audio • $12.00 / NLE-19v • 45 min Video • $19.95

HERBS FOR IMMUNITY, with Renee Ponder, Master Herbalist. Learn how to rid the body of mucus, toxins, waste, and parasites, as well as the importance of a regular program with herbs. Learn to distinguish the quality of the herbs and how to integrate diet with herbal protocol. This lecture is for all interested in prevention and for those with a compromised immune systems. With over 21 years of experience, Renee is renowned for her simple protocols and exceptional herbal formulas. A pioneer in the field, she has acquired expertise in the use of herbs for the immune system. NLE-20a • 45 min Audio • $12.00 / NLE-20v • 45 min Video • $19.95

HEALTH, HEALING AND WHOLENESS: AN EMBODIED WORKSHOP FOR WOMEN, with Arisika Razak. Join us for an ecstatic exploration of our wholeness as women. Using movement, sound, ritual and yoga to create a safe container for calling the Divine, telling our stories, and honoring the body in all its diversity.We will use authentic and natural movement to reclaim our creativity; release old traumas and stress; tone and strengthen the body; and re-member and ground our power. Come gather in

sacred play as we celebrate and honor our connection to Life, Eros, Power, and Creativity. Arisika Razak, RN, CNM, MPH, Certified Kripalu Yoga Instructor, is an Associate Professor of Women's Spirituality at the California Institute of Integral Studies. She has been a midwife, healer and spiritual dancer for over 30 years. NLE-21a • 45 min Audio • $12.00 / NLE-21v • 45 min Video • $19.95

LIFE CHANGING ISSUES FOR WOMEN, with Kathleen O'Bannon. A Certified Nutrition Consultant, she will discuss simple solutions to hormonal imbalances for women. Health problems such as migraines, bloating, fatigue, food cravings, weight gain, hot flashes, anxiety, depression, and just plain crankiness can be related to hormonal imbalances.We will discuss menopause, perimenopause, PMS and more.Women, as young as 35, can be affected by these hormonal changes. Find the answers you have been searching for and regain your youthfulness. An internationally acclaimed expert on women's health issues, TV and Radio personality, and author of six books, O'Bannon has helped thousands of women overcome symptoms related to female hormonal imbalance. NLE-22a • 45 min Audio • $12.00 / NLE-22v • 45 min Video • $19.95

MAN-WOMAN MADE EASY - NO KIDDING! With Kristina Catalina. Learn the untold secrets of how to have happy, satisfied and gratified women in your life. Discover what it takes to have men feel like a hero around you, and want to do anything for you. Learn the simple, yet profound truths why most relationships don't work and how to turn them around instantly and effortlessly utilizing the gifts you were born with as a man and a woman. Catalina is a Relationship Humorist. She has had her own talk radio show and has taught seminars internationally for 18 years.With her clarity, wit and humor she inspires people to have more FUN with their differences. NLE-23a • 45 min Audio • $12.00 / NLE-23v • 45 min Video • $19.95

SEXUAL HEALING, with Raja Selvam. Sexual trauma and abuse can wound us deeply leaving scars that are physical, emotional, psychological, and spiritual. In this workshop we will explore together tools we may use to harness and transform the energies of trauma. We will do this through guided, group awareness exercises and video case material. NLE-01a • 45 min Audio • $12.00 / NLE-01v • 45 min Video • $19.95 NLE-24a • 45 min Audio • $12.00 / NLE-24v • 45 min Video • $19.95

SACRED UNION: PATH TO SELF-ASCENSION, with Sri Ram Kaa & Kira Raa. You are your greatest life story. Joy is a choice, the building block of self-ascension. Learn how to transform your daily life, with or without a partner, into an experience of divine sacred union, where every day is an adventure in gratitude. Sri Ram Kaa & Kira Raa, with Archangel Zadkiel's guidance, will teach down-to-earth practices that lead to a self-ascended state and will address your personal roadblocks to expansion. . Sri Ram Kaa is a gifted healer and therapist. Kira Raa is a popular clairvoyant and intuitive TV guest. Published authors, they offer spiritual coaching, group workshops, and retreats for sacred writers. NLE-01a • 45 min Audio • $12.00 / NLE-25v • 45 min Video • $19.95 NLE-25a • 45 min Audio • $12.00 / NLE-20v • 45 min Video • $19.95

PARENTING OURSELVES AND OUR CHILDREN FOR SELF ESTEEM, SELF WORTH AND SELF CONFIDENCE, with Art Martin. Provide a functional family and a foundation for success and well being. We have to change the parental model or we will treat our children in the same manner we were treated by our parents. Our children will end up with the following statistics as we have unless we rectify our parents' mistakes. 7 out of 10 children were rejected before they were born, 2 out of the 10 were rejected in childhood, and only 1 out of 10 has a chance of having a reasonable future.We will demonstrate a process to release the effect of the negative parental model in both parents and children. A thought-provoking speaker, Martin developed Neuro/Cellular Repatterning and is trained in Chinese/Tibetan medicine and other therapies. NLE-26a • 45 min Audio • $12.00 / NLE-26v • 45 min Video • $19.95

HEMP FOODS: LEARN ALL ABOUT HEMP SEED NUTRITION, with John W. Roulac. Discover why hemp seed is the world's most nutritious seed in the world. Rich in Omega-3, vitamin E and protein, Hemp seed and oil has a light nutty flavor and has been used as a food in China for over 6,000 years. Today hemp is found in food bars, breads, cereal chips, salad dressings, nutritional oils, ice cream, nut butters, etc. Learn how to use hemp oil, shelled hempseed, and hemp protein powder in a variety of delicious recipes. Roulac is an advocate for holistic living and author of 4 books including Hemp Horizons and Backyard Composting. He is a founder of Nutiva-America's leading hemp foods brand, Harmonious Technologies, and Forests Forever. NLE-27a • 45 min Audio • $12.00 / NLE-27v • 45 min Video • $19.95

SPIRITUAL NUTRITION: AN INTRODUCTION TO THE HEALING PROPERTIES OF FOOD AND HERBS, with Marie Fairchild. This lecture will introduce you to the concept of spiritual nutrition. Discover how the healing energy of certain food, herbs and minerals can increase your vitality, your health, and your longevity. Between Heaven and Earth there flows constant energy. Traditional Chinese Medicine is based on the precept that all life is infused with a universal energy known as Chi. One way to absorb this energy is through the food we eat. Learn about the energetic properties of foods for the body / mind / spirit. Fairchild is a certified nutrition consultant and owner of Apple Lakes Nutritional Therapies in San Francisco.She is practiced in the art of Chinese herbology and Feng Shui. NLE-28a • 45 min Audio • $12.00 / NLE-28v • 45 min Video • $19.95

THE METABOLIC PLAN, with Stephen Cherniske. Internationally renowned biochemist Stephen Cherniske presents a new paradigm that radically alters our understanding of the aging process. Cherniske shows that the human body is naturally endowed with astonishing powers of renewal, self-repair, and regeneration. Drawing from his new book, The Metabolic Plan Cherniske takes you step-by-step through the process of restoring the body's ability to repair its own cells, enabling one to grow biologically "younger" at any age. Cherniske, a nutritional biochemist with more than thirty years of experience, directed the nation's first FDA-licensed clinical laboratory specializing in nutrition testing. His other works include: The DHEA Breakthrough, and Caffeine Blues. NLE-29a • 45 min Audio • $12.00 / NLE-29v • 45 min Video • $19.95

TANTRIC HARMONICS: EMPOWERING THE HEALING VOICE, with Sophia Roberts. The voice is a potent tool of transformation when freed of the blockages to dynamic expression. Explore the use of toning and Mongolian Overtone Chanting to energize, integrate and align our chakras, tuning the "inner flute" that allows us to be more perfect instruments of spirit. With our empowered voices, we will practice healing and opening the heart to ourselves, each other and our Mother Earth. Roberts calls herself a songhealer, and dedicates her music and teaching to empowering the healing, transformative and creative voice. Her tenth CD, Chakra Healing Chants, is now available. Visit her at www.songhealer.com NLE-30a • 45 min Audio • $12.00 / NLE-30v • 45 min Video • $19.95

RETURN TO THE MAGIC OF FULL CIRCLE HEALING THROUGH THE VIBRATIONAL POWER OF CHANTING, with Belinda Farrell & Joy Metcalfe. Join Belinda Farrell and Joy Metcalfe in a Multi-level experience exploring new and ancient pathways to healing. Return to the power of now. Experience the healing of self-forgiveness. Create a quantum leap in your DNA structure. Continue your transformation into light. Metcalfe is an internationally known Medical Intuitive and Teacher; and was voted Best Reiki Master Teacher by Share Guide Magazine. Farrell is a Master Hypnotherapist, Radio and Film personality. Huna Practitioner and Chanter of Ancient Hawaiian healing. NLE-31a • 45 min Audio • $12.00 / NLE-31v • 45 min Video • $19.95

A SOUND WAY TO A BETTER YOU! with James Phillips. Would you like to focus like a laser? Could you use a tenminute power nap to rejuvenate during your hectic day? Having trouble switching gears when you get home from work? Would you like a deeper meditation to better communicate with your spirit guides? Come see and hear the amazing new Total Mind Audio Technology that will transform your life to a Better You! Phillips lectures extensively on the benefits of the Total Mind Audio Technology and is a fully accredited trainer with the Monroe Institute in Virginia. He has a background in worldwide film and television productions, including the series: "Food of the Pharaohs". NLE-32a • 45 min Audio • $12.00 / NLE-32v • 45 min Video • $19.95

CHAKRA TONING AND VOICING YOUR SOUL, with Wayne Perry. Join internationally acclaimed sound healer Wayne Perry for an illuminating and entertaining journey into chakra toning. Discover the secrets to using the natural vibrational healing power within your voice to clear, strengthen and balance the chakras and voice your soul. Consisting of vibrational energy, we can easily learn to master our personal frequencies with sound, toning and vocal harmonics. This presentation will include a demonstration of regenerative sound and a group "chakra chant".Founder and director of the Sound Therapy Center of Los Angeles, Perry's unique talents have been featured on CBS News, CNN, Strange Universe and The Roseanne Show. NLE-33a • 45 min Audio • $12.00 / NLE-33v • 45 min Video • $19.95

HOW YOUR BELIEFS CREATE YOUR REALITY - AN EXPERIENTIAL INQUIRY, with Lion Goodman. How do you create your life? The Avatar course teaches the fundamental mechanics of creating, based on the simple truth that your beliefs cause you to create or attract the situations and events you experience in your life. In this experiential inquiry, you can begin to explore your beliefs, and discover exercises that can be directly applied to improving your life. Goodman is a licensed teacher of The Avatar Course, a 9-day training for awakening and enlightenment. He is also a life coach, a published author and inspirational public speaker. NLE-34a • 45 min Audio • $12.00 / NLE-34v • 45 min Video • $19.95

DISTANCE HEALING: RECENT RESEARCH, with Francesca McCartney, Ph.D. Findings from a recent research project funded and conducted at the Institute of Noetic Sciences. Distance healing and intuitive communication may both be seen as non-linear, non-local systems of information exchange. The potential exists for email information content to hold intentional sensorial resonance; and for this type of email to be used as a provider of energy information that can be utilized as a medium for distance healing. When a receptive person reads an email, they can receive the emotional/cognitive content of intentionally encapsulated healing energy. McCartney, Ph.D. founded the Academy of Intuitive Studies and Intuition Medicine® in 1984 in Sausalito. An intuitive counselor, teacher and author. NLE-35a • 45 min Audio • $12.00 / NLE-35v • 45 min Video • $19.95

USING YOUR INTUITION TO LIVE PASSIONATELY, with Susan Stuart, Ph.D. We each possess the innate ability to live each day in joy. During the next Cosmic phase you will be invited to explore your unique potential for passion. Susan has the Intuitive awareness, developed through years of working with clients, to guide you through the door to your "Passion Potential".Take an opportunity to view your future. Stuart is a professional Intuitive Counselor who has over 26 years experi-

ence in her field. She is clairvoyant, clairaudient and is a trance channel. In 1981 Stuart founded the Intuitive Development Institute which offers Intuitive Life Descriptions, Intuitive Counseling and Medical Intuitive Training. NLE-36a • 45 min Audio • $12.00 / NLE-36v • 45 min Video • $19.95

THE POWER OF TOUCH: CHAMPISSAGE IN THE 21ST CENTURY, with Narandra Mehta. Learn the origins of Indian Head Massage, currently Britain's most popular complementary therapy. Discover how this ancient touch system can benefit you. Experience how Indian Champissage beautifully combines physical and subtle energy massage to help all kinds of stress- related symptoms. Witness a powerful demonstration of this treatment and give yourself a session at Narendra's booth. Narendra Mehta is Principal of the London Centre of Indian Champissage. He has been practicing bodywork for over 20 years and leading Indian Champissage training courses for 15 years. His published works include Indian Head Massage and The Art of Indian Face Massage. NLE-37a • 45 min Audio • $12.00 / NLE-37v • 45 min Video • $19.95

FINDING LOVE: RELATIONSHIP SUCCESS FOR SINGLES, with Carol Daly. Find the life and love of your dreams. Making choices in alignment with your values and life purpose allows you to experience relationship and personal fulfillment. Come and learn the 10 Principles of Conscious Dating and personalize them with your values, life purpose, personal attributes and gifts.With this blueprint for success, the "Law of Attraction" can work for you and your future partner. Daly is a Relationship Coach, Rapid Eye Practitioner, and Hypnotherapist located in Los Altos. She specializes in releasing self-defeating thoughts, beliefs, and patterns, thus saving time, reducing frustration and achieving goals. NLE-38a • 45 min Audio • $12.00 / NLE-38v • 45 min Video • $19.95

EAT YOURSELF SEX: ELECTRICALLY AVAILABLE FOODS, with Denie Heistand. This fun informative workshop will give you insights into how you can eat yourself sexy, increase your libido, achieve your optimal weight, and have more energy. Denie is a world authority on the electrical workings of body. His talk will give you the tools you need to bring more conscious awareness to the nutritional needs of your body, heart and soul. Guaranteed to be an on-the-edge presentation that will wake you up and motivate you to be all that you are. Denie Heistend is the author of Electrical Nutrition and Journey to Truth, founder of the International Institute of Vibrational Wellness and the Electrical Nutrition Professional Company. NLE-39a • 45 min Audio • $12.00 / NLE-39v • 45 min Video • $19.95

THE MAGIC OF INTERSPECIES COMMUNICATION, with Penelope Smith. Expand your conscious, harmonious interaction with other species. Discover how animals communicate and understand us, and what prevents humans from receiving their messages. Learn about animals' intelligence and how to help animals through direct communication with them and how animals help us to integrate body, mind and spirit. Advance from human-centeredness to interspecies, all-being communion. Smith, world-renowned pioneer in the field of interspecies communication, is the author of the popular, classic books on the subject, Animal Talk and When Animals Speak (available in many languages) and editor of the quarterly journal, Species Link. NLE-40a • 45 min Audio • $12.00 / NLE-40v • 45 min Video • $19.95

UNDERSTANDING ENERGY AND YOUR RELATIONSHIP, with Phyllis Light, Ph.D. Dr. Light discusses how deeply our energy affects our friends and loved ones. Key subconscious patterns are presented < ways we use our energy unconsciously to manipulate others — and how to overcome those patterns. You will learn about the fourth dimension and the true energetic nature of reality, and how to tap into your true spiritual power in order to experience winning in your relationships. Light is a teacher, counselor, and author of Prince Charming Lives: Finding the Love of Your Life. In her work, "Telepathic Healing," she helps people clear negative programming to the depths of the subconscious mind, while infusing their essence with a higher octave of light and spiritual energy. NLE-41a • 45 min Audio • $12.00 / NLE-41v • 45 min Video • $19.95

FORCE AND FEELING: THE ENERGETICS OF PERSONALITY AND SEXUAL CHEMISTRY, with Julie Motz. Each of us has a fundamental energy pattern that determines both the structure of our personality and whom we are drawn to sexually and emotionally. This lecture will describe the four basic patterns and help you determine if you are a Boundary Maker, a Defender, a Negotiator or a Pacifier. Discover what this means for your romantic future and for making your current relationship exciting, fulfilling and successful. Motz is an internationally known energy healer and author of the book Hands of Life. She is cofounder of Chemistry Plus, a matchmaking service that guarantees sexual and emotional compatibility. NLE-42a • 45 min Audio • $12.00 / NLE-42v • 45 min Video • $19.95

HAPPINESS IS NOT AN INDIVIDUAL MATTER: OUR ENGAGEMENT WITH LIFE, with Gary Gach. Explore the radical, this worldly dimensions of the teachings of the Buddha, as applied in our secular world today. Topics will include service (hospices, for example), deep ecology (our planet is ourselves), gender equity (whatever happened to the Buddhas mother?), erasing racism (making the invisible visible), social justice (knowing a better way to catch a snake) and peace (yes, peace). Learn how Buddhism brings us the understanding and solidity so needed in todays society. Gach is an American Book Award-winning author of over six books, with works in 125+ magazines. NLE-43a • 45 min Audio • $12.00 / NLE-43v • 45 min Video • $19.95

HOW TO COMMUNICATE WITH YOUR ANGELS, with Reverend Mary. Rev. Mary will share some of her own profound experiences as a Channel & Instrument For God after her own

Near Death Experience. Hear first hand, information Rev. Mary channeled from The Angelic Team. Learn how to listen and communicate with your own Angels. Find out how prayer & meditations link you with God and your Angels to give connections with powerful spiritual energies. Bring your own questions for channeled answers. Rev. Mary is a Professional Psychic, Trance Medium, Intuitive, Clairvoyant, Ordained Minister, who shares her God-given gifts with others via Angelic Communications, Tarot, and Trance Channeling. Her abilities developed after a series of Near Death Experiences. NLE-44a • 45 min Audio • $12.00 / NLE-44v • 45 min Video • $19.95

DEEPENING LOVE AND PASSION AS WE AGE, with Dr. Victoria Lee. News Flash! When it comes to passionate sex, don't trust anyone under 30! Dr. Victoria Lee's survey of workshop participants and sex therapy clients reveals that the most passionate lovemaking we are all capable of is more available to us in maturity than in youth. A sacred approach to sexuality opens the heart and frees the body and soul for the ecstatic experiences we were made for. This lecture will teach you three secrets of lifelong passion. Dr. Lee is a clinical psychologist and sex therapist who lectures and trains audiences internationally in sacred sexuality. Her book, Ecstatic Lovemaking: An Intimate Guide to Soulful Sex, opens new and exciting doors to Lifelong passion. NLE-45a • 45 min Audio • $12.00 / NLE-45v • 45 min Video • $19.95

GAIA'S REMEDY: NEW HOPE FOR OUR DYING OAKS, with Lee Klinger, Ph.D. From a Gaian perspective, forests are considered the "lungs" of the planet. Yet, as more and more pockets of dying oak trees appear in our native woodlands, many of us wonder whether humans have stressed our forests to their limits of tolerance. Are the lungs of the earth about to collapse? The concepts and complexity of Gaia shed new light and offer a new cure for our dying trees. Dr. Klinger, Senior Scientist at the Institute of Noetic Sciences in Petaluma, California, is recognized as one of the worlds' leading scholars in global ecology and Gaia theory. NLE-46a • 45 min Audio • $12.00 / NLE-46v • 45 min Video • $19.95

GREEN INVESTING IN LOCAL COMPANIES, with Mark Perlmutter. Mark Perlmutter teaches average Americans to get in on the ground floor of green technologies i.e zero emission cars and medically inspired ergonomic furniture. Products of the future are being funded today using small public offerings. These offerings helped companies like Ben & Jerry's and Real Goods grow to become leaders. Come hear how to make a profit while making a difference. Perlmutter, a financial advisor for more than twenty years, is the founder of the MicroAngels Investor Education Club, and teaches how to foster responsible sustainable businesses by investing locally (not globally) and "provide profits while making a difference!" NLE-47a • 45 min Audio • $12.00 / NLE-47v • 45 min Video • $19.95

WHY POLY-MVA MAY BE THE BEST THERAPY AROUND, with Ken Walker. Ken Walker will introduce Poly-MVA, an alternative super nutrient. This amazing product has already shown extraordinary healing abilities for degenerative diseases, including cancer. Walker will reveal much information on today's cancer situation. With the loss of his wife to cancer Dr. Sanchez vowed to relentlessly search for a cure. He soon became CEO of several pharmaceutical distributors, which eventually led him to Poly-MVA, a nontoxic cancer alternative product that he wishes to announce to the world. NLE-48a • 45 min Audio • $12.00 / NLE-48v • 45 min Video • $19.95

RADICAL NATURE: A MIND OF IT'S OWN? with Christian de Quincey, Ph.D. Christian helps us rediscover our deep kinship with the natural world. Explore our culture's "dominant story," enshrined in both science and religion, and open to a "new" and ancient story. The split between humanity and the rest of the world is rooted in our metaphysical beliefs about the nature of matter and mind, and the relationship between spirit and body. Heal that split using the wisdom of feeling and the power of story. Quincey, an international speaker on consciousness, cosmology, and spirituality, is a professor of philosophy and consciousness studies at JFK University, and managing editor of IONS Review, published by the Institute of Noetic Sciences. NLE-49a • 45 min Audio • $12.00 / NLE-49v • 45 min Video • $19.95

THE BLISS FACTOR, with Norman McVey, Ph.D. What we most need on an hourly basis is a vacation or mental holiday from stress.We yearn to lift our spirits. Get Excited about music again with 5th Dimensional Sound CD's & Systems, the InnerQuest System designed to create deep states of meditation and sexual/spiritual healing. Learn how to transform both private and public spaces into a sanctuary with The Atlantis HighLife System, a high-tech Feng Shui system designed to release stress and raise vitality! McVea, is director of research and development for ORI, LLC., and the inventor of Life Energy Amplifiers⁰. He has authored 4 books, including The Bliss Factor numerous audiotape programs including over 35 Self Processing programs. NLE-50a • 45 min Audio • $12.00 / NLE-50v • 45 min Video • $19.95

VELVET THE APPROACHABILITY FACTOR, with Pepper Freye, Ph.D. In this difficult marketplace you need an edge up on the competition. Wearing velvet can make an extreme difference for people to do business with you. Psychologically a client, friend, co-worker, potential mate, etc., will find you more attractive and approachable if you wear velvet! Learn 8 reasons why this is so! Pepper is the owner of Saucy Goddesswear. She is a speaker on the psychology of color and has a Ph.D. in Counseling from the University of Metaphysics, Los Angeles. NLE-51a • 45 min Audio • $12.00 / NLE-51v • 45 min Video • $19.95

ALL ABOUT EMOTIONAL FREEDOM TECHNIQUES™ (EFT), with Michael Reins. A psychological version of acupuncture without needles, EFT is known to significantly decrease or eliminate the effects of trauma, anger, fear, sadness, worry, cravings, physical discomforts and to enhance your performance in areas such as learning and sports performance. It's easy to learn and use. Today, witness the miracles of EFT as Michael Reins teaches it and you use it! Reins teaches and practices Emotional Freedom Techniques™ and was personally trained by Gary Craig, the founder of EFT. He works as a Life Coach and Psychotherapist. NLE-52a • 45 min Audio • $12.00 / NLE-52v • 45 min Video • $19.95

THE VEILS OF ILLUSION, with Rich Work. True healing comes from within. Personally conquering cancer, heart disease, chronic fatigue, asthma, and mercury poisoning, he guides you to awaken the healing power within, lift the veils of illusion, reclaim your empowerment, move beyond limitations, and celebrate life. Rich demonstrates the simplicity of healing and takes you on a powerful journey of understanding the divine nature of your being, including Awaken to the Healer Within. He is president of Harmonics International and founder of Symmetry International. He is also the administrator of Symmetry 21-day Transformational Cocoons where miracles happen. NLE-53a • 45 min Audio • $12.00 / NLE-53v • 45 min Video • $19.95

WORK SYMMETRY: THE BREATH OF LIFE, with Ann Marie. Ann Marie shares powerful techniques she used to heal her body and her life. Personally conquering multiple sclerosis, she activated the healing power within, by moving the body's natural Rhythms of Rejuvenation. Her 21-day transformational cocoon has exceeded expectations. Those challenged with AIDS, cancer, diabetes, depression, drug and alcohol addictions, allergies, etc., rediscover vital health in just 21-days. Ann is the founder of Symmetry Ministry International and creator of Harmonic Vibrational Products and Harmonic Synchronistic Attunements. She is also co-author of Awaken to the Healer Within and Director of Symmetry 21- day Transformational Cocoons. NLE-54a • 45 min Audio • $12.00 / NLE-54v • 45 min Video • $19.95

BRINGING LIFE TO WATER AND YOUR BODY, with Fred Van Liew. Learn the science behind E Crystal technology and the latest in water revitalization. Protection from environmental chaos is now possible. Learn how to affordably protect your body, your home, and your work environment. Learn from the world's leading expert in the field of water and water appliances. Fred has taught on water technologies, purification, and all forms of health care for nearly twenty-two years. He is founder of Essential Water & Air and lectures at Karl Parker Healing Seminars and has published in numerous journals. NLE-55a • 45 min Audio • $12.00 / NLE-55v • 45 min Video • $19.95

BIO-FEEDBACK, HEALTH, IMMUNITY AND YOU, with Theresa Palmer. Bio-feedback screening is a painless process utilizing the meridians used in acupuncture to measure aspects of your health. In this presentation, you can learn ways to improve your energy and overall health. Bio-feedback can reveal how certain foods affect your metabolism. You may learn how unknown sensitivities are interconnected with other conditions that impact how you're feeling. You will learn more when you see this demonstration. Palmer worked 8 years in alternative medicine prior to earning her naturopathic degree in 1995. Her focus is educating her clients to be empowered in handling their health issues. NLE-56a • 45 min Audio • $12.00 / NLE-56v • 45 min Video • $19.95

THE URANTIA BOOK: A LOVE LETTER FROM THE UNIVERSE, with Paula Thompson. A revelation to humanity from the headquarters of a trillion inhabited worlds. The Urantia Book provides a panoramic view of God, cosmology, life after death, mankind's evolution and history, and Jesus' entire life and teachings (including the missing years). This book can restore selfesteem, return hope, increase personal peace and joy, expand insight, and enhance cosmic wisdom and understanding. Paula Thompson currently serves on the executive boards of two Urantia oriented nonprofits, for 27 years she has successfully taught these amazing concepts to others. NLE-57a • 45 min Audio • $12.00 / NLE-57v • 45 min Video • $19.95

COACHING? SO WHAT THE HECK IS COACHING? with Rosie Kuhn, Ph.D. This is an opportunity to acquaint yourself with some unique and powerful skills and tools, which distinguish coaching from other forms of personal development work. Coaching through management opportunities, therapeutic sessions, sales work, family dialogue, etc., produces great results where a desired outcome through conversation is intended. Relating from the spiritual nature of our essential being is the underlying principle of this work. Kuhn, a graduate of the Institute of Transpersonal Psychology, facilitates training programs in transformational coaching, and spiritual guidance. Her private practice integrates coaching, spiritual guidance, and therapeutic skills. NLE-58a • 45 min Audio • $12.00 / NLE-58v • 45 min Video • $19.95

HYPNOBIRTHING®: A CELEBRATION OF LIFE, with Yvonne Schwab. Why is giving birth so medicalized and/or painful? Why wasn't it in the past? How can we reconnect to the power of our Birthing Bodies? Birthing was never supposed to be painful or traumatic. It is a rite of passage in which the mother should be honored and the baby revered. Join this discussion and find the answer to these and other questions about birthing by using HypnoBirthing®, The Mongan Method. Schwab is a Certified Hypnotherapist, a Certified HypnoBirthing® Practitioner, and a Certified Spiritual Counselor. She teaches Advanced Pain Management and Hypnosis for Childbirth at the Center for Hypnotherapy Training and practices in San Jose. NLE-59a • 45 min Audio • $12.00 / NLE-59v • 45 min Video • $19.95

THE EARTH SPEAKS TO THOSE THAT LISTEN, with Christine Wallace, Ph.D. Through breathtaking drumming and song, Christine speaks directly to the Spirit within you. She will teach you practical insights into effective and profound prayer and meditation. Utilizing Native American spirituality, she can show you how to understand and interpret the messages and answers to your deepest questions provided by Nature. Christine is revered as a Thunder Being by Native Americans: a Spiritual Leader, Intuitive, Medium and Catalyst for major world change. Wallace is recognized the world over though her CDs, radio shows and guest appearances on Seeing Beyond where she is featured regularly. A gifted Medium, Psychic, and Spiritual Teacher. NLE-60a • 45 min Audio • $12.00 / NLE-60v • 45 min Video • $19.95

THE HAZARDS OF ELECTROMAGNETIC RADIATION
THE HAZARDS OF ELECTROMAGNETIC SMOG, POW-ERLINES, ELFS, TELEVISIONS AND VDTS. Articles on EMAG smog, microwave radiation concerns, minimizing your exposure, invisible pollution, book review, Pandora revisited, RF effects on cells, health hazards of EMAG fields, estimating ELF exposure, sixth sense compass, high-voltage dangers, EMAGs and leukemia, EMAG allergies, cancer risk, video display terminals and miscarriages, cutting PC radiation risk, VDT risks, EMAG and health, TV and X-Ray radiation, X-Ray risk, and more. EMAG-01 • 169 pages • illustrated • 8 1/2 x 11 • stapled binding • $25.00
THE HAZARDS OF MICROWAVE OVENS, CELLULAR PHONE TECHNOLOGY, PROTECTION FROM ELEC-TROMAGNETIC WAVES AND HEALING ELECROMAG-NETICS. Articles on microwave ovens, possible danger of eating microwaved food, microwaved pork can kill, food vending hazards, sectrol group, cellular tower protests, cellular and digital dilemma, enhanced specialized radio, microwave tower threat, cellular siting investigation, EMF detectors, the SomaShield, the Eye Guard, Clarus systems, the NoRad monitor shield, sea plants, the Rife Report, the universal microscope, life saving machines, cross currents article, the body electric, electron distribution, and more. EMAG-02 • 171 pages • illustrated • 8 1/2 x 11 • stapled binding • $25.00
SUPPORTING EVIDENCE OF ELF AND MICROWAVE HAZARDS. Articles on biological effects of electromagnetic and extremely low frequency (ELF) waves, a US Senate report on radiation and health, effects of microwaves on neurons, human electromagnetic symbiosis, the effects of weak ELFs on monkeys, biological effects of microwaves, bio-effects and health, bio-effects on EEG, supporting results, and more. EMAG-03 • 136 pages • illustrated • 8 1/2 x 11 • stapled binding • $21.00
A SYNOPSIS OF HAZARDOUS ELECTROMAGNETIC RADIATION, compiled by Tedd St. Rain. One each of the preceding 3 chapters (EMAG-01 through EMAG-03) combined into one book and made available at a special price. EMAG-91 • 476 pages • illustrated • 8 1/2 x 11 • stapled binding • $62.00
NIKOLA TESLA AND HIS INVENTIONS
Overview of Nikola Tesla's Work. Articles on Nikola Tesla and some of the technology he provided to the world. Topics include operation of a Tesla coil, wireless transmission, bladeless turbine, rotary heat motor, Marconi, acoustic diver beacon, an alleged channeling of Tesla. Also the Article "On Increasing Human Energy" from The Century Illustrated Monthly Magazine, June 1900. Tesla gives his insights on human energy. Topics include harnessing the sun's energy, the 3 ways of increasing human energy, the burning of nitrogen, the art of teleutomatics, waste in iron manufacture, age of aluminum, electrical oscillation. Also "Nikola Tesla: The Dreamer. His 3-Day Airship and More" from the World Today, Vol. XXI, No 8, Feb 1912. Topics include a 3-day ship to Europe, dynamo-electric machinery, news reports, patents, miscellaneous articles, and more. TESLA-01 • 116 pages • 8 1/2 x 11 • stapled binding • $18.00
SOME PATENT APPLICATIONS AND ASSORTED RESEARCH ARTICLES OF NIKOLA TESLA. Patent applications in Tesla's own handwriting and related patent copies. Topics include valvular conduits, producing high-frequency oscillating currents, radio-signalling systems. Also includes research articles on the world's greatest engineer, AC, high-frequencies, ball lightning, an experimental receiver, and more. TESLA-02 • 95 pages • 8 1/2 x 11 • stapled binding • $15.00
NIKOLA TESLA NEWSPAPER AND JOURNAL ARTI-CLES. Over 100 articles written by and about Nikola Tesla. Off the internet, with sources from newspapers, electrical journals, research articles, etc. Topics include wireless transmission, high-frequency currents, AC, dynamos, bladeless turbine, the moon's rotation, induction circuits, radio power and much more. TESLA-03 • 214 pages • 8 1/2 x 11 • stapled binding • $33.00
Nikola Tesla: Lectures, Patents and Articles. A complete collection of Tesla's work in three sections, including lecture transcripts, a complete list of patents, and articles he wrote for various publications. Topics include motors, generators, transmission of power, lighting, high-frequency apparatus, radio, turbines, and much more. 4-up on a page, but still readable. TESLA-04 • 213 pages • 8 1/2 x 11 • stapled binding • $33.00
AN OVERVIEW OF NIKOLA TESLA AND HIS INVEN-TIONS, compiled by Tedd St. Rain. One each of the preceding 4 chapters (TESLA-01 through TESLA-04) combined into one book and made available at a special price. TESLA-91 • 638 pages • illustrated • 8 1/2 x 11 • stapled binding • $83.00
FREE ENERGY RESEARCH
ELECTROMAGNETIC FIELD THEORIES, BACK-GROUND ON FREE ENERGY RESEARCHERS, THE MYSTERIOUS AIRSHIPS OF THE 1800S, JOHN KEELEY AND HIS AMAZING DISCOVERIES, A HISTORY OF PERPETUAL MOTION MACHINES, AND MICHAEL FARADAY'S FREE ENERGY MACHINE. Articles on odic-activity rays, the zone of silence, the Higgs field, the void theory, double-helix pyramid beam, on Richard Clem's over-unity

engine, an engine that runs itself, Hyde energy generator, Swiss M-L Testavistatika energy converter, alpha and gamma ray therapy, alchemist 1956, early UFO sightings in the 1800's, the 1896 sky show, analysis of the 1897 airships, great airship inventors, Pennington's airship, Dellschau and his esoteric book, Mymza and the airships of the 1850's, John Ernst Keely, the structure of the molecule, secrets of 1888, run on the stock market, the Vedas, mantras, mandalas, the Krell helmet, sympathetic vibration, the neutral centre, amplitude of force, acoustophoresis. Ernst Chladni, splitting molecules producing energy, triune and mono-polarity, aqueous disintegration, John Keely's mystery motor, perpetual motion machine, mineral disintegration, consequences of Keely's death, the Keely myth and motor hoax, perpetual motion machines, memo from the US patent office, the Charles Redheffer perpetual motion machine, perpetual motion of the second kind, new thermal engine, chronology of government suppression of inventions, synopsis of books on free energy, free energy physics, Bruce DePalma, magnetic motors, extraction of energy from space, the Faraday disc, homopolar free energy generator, and more. FREE-01 • 155 pages • 8 1/2 x 11 • stapled binding • $24.00
A HISTORY OF WALTER RUSSELL AND ZERO-POINT-ENERGY, AN OVERVIEW OF ZERO POINT ENERGY, REVIEW OF ZPE AND FREE ENERGY, HANS COLER AND A NEW SOURCE OF POWER. Articles on the macrobiotic genius of Walter Russell, Russell and Zero Point Energy, interesting article side-bars, Zero Point Energy, free energy from magnetism, the leftovers of nothing, the energetic vacuum, government suppression of emerging energy technology, Zero Point Energy, Free Energy theory, experimental progress, new devices, Hans Coler, the Magnetstromapparat, details of the Stromerzeuger, F. Modershn, professor Kloss, Professor Schumann, Dr. Frohlich, and more. FREE-02 • 164 pages • 8 1/2 x 11 • stapled binding • $25.00
INTRODUCTION TO SCALAR ELECTROMAGNETICS, WATER-SPLITTING HYDROGEN POWERED CARS, SOLAR POWER AND ENERGY INDEPENDENCE, COLD NUCLEAR FUSION: FACT OR FANTASY? Articles on warnings on Scalar and Tesla experiments, scalar translators, scalar technology and a unified field equation, background for pursuing scalar electromagnetics, omni-directional longitudinal scalar wave translator, the mysterious power source of 1931 car, electric-powered autos, new auto runs on human urine, Stanely Meyer's water-splitting electric cell, NeonLite electric transformer, fuel free engines, Sam Leach's box, hydrogen-powered car, gasoline purifier, Nazi research, present-day power generation, a solar energy primer, breakthroughs in solar technology, polymeric light and power conversion, an older "real goods" listing, cold nuclear fusion, chemistry of the Utah reactor, magnetic confinement, cold fusion in condensed matter, kitchen table fusion, electrochemically induced fusion in Deuterium, a guide to uncommon metals, syntrophic transducer, cold fusion mystery solved, ball lightning and fusion energy, and more. FREE-03 • 104 pages • 8 1/2 x 11 • stapled binding • $16.00
A SUMMARY OF FREE ENERGY AND PERPETUAL MOTION RESEARCHERS, Compiled by Tedd St. Rain. One each of the preceding 3 chapters (FREE-01 through FREE-03) combined into one book and made available at a special price. FREE-91 • 477 or 423 pages • illustrated • 8 1/2 x 11 • stapled binding • $64.00 or $55.00
ANTI-GRAVITY RESEARCH
FUNDEMENTAL NEWTONIAN PHYSICS, EINSTEIN'S RELATIVITY AND GRAVITATION, REVIEW OF CON-TEMPORARY COSMIC PHYSICS, INTERSTELLAR ASTRONOMY AND SPACE FLIGHT, COSMOLOGY AND INTERSTELLAR ASTRONOMY. Articles on roll over Isaac Newton, 2nd law of gravitation, a challenge to relativity, Earth's center of gravity, ion-trusters, relativitivist limitations, satellite verifies theory of gravity, gravity testing, Newtonian gravitational constant, sensational physics, conference on cosmic rays, good vibrations, absence of gravity, weight of photons, oscillating gravity field, on new moons near Earth, zero-gravity tests, fluid testing, astrodynamics, lunar gravity, gravitational speed, interstellar molecules, unsteady universe, particle creation, gravity detection, astrodynamics, and more. GRAV-01 • 153 pages • 8 1/2 x 11 • stapled binding • $23.00
CONFERENCES AND AWARDS ON GRAVITY, BACK-GROUND FOR ANTI-GRAVITY RESEARCH, GRAVITY AND ANTI-GRAVITY EXPLORATION, MAN-MADE EARTH-BASED UFO PROPULSION, GYROSCOPIC ANTI-GRAVITY RESEARCH, JOHN BIGELOW'S SAUCER TECHNOLOGY. Articles and synopsis on a series of conferences that the Gravity Research Foundation put on in 1961. Includes guest and award categories, handouts, reverse gravity, anti-gravity, conquest of space, starship engines, light flashes, space anomalies, saucer's secret, Russian craft, anti-gravity, Gauss scientific journal, Gravity Research Foundation, the case for anti-gravity, gravitational theory, on UFOs, the occult Reich, foo fighters, UFOs: alien or man-made, how to build a saucer, defying gravity, Frank Chase, Otis T. Carr, OTC Enterprises, Joseph Newman gyroscopic theory, Japanese anti-gravity. mass of spinning rotors, saucer technology, spinning rotors, heating plasma, magneto hydrodynamic generation, ion propulsion, hand-scribbled notes, and more. GRAV-02 • 174 pages • 8 1/2 x 11 • stapled binding • $26.00
ELECTRO-GRAVITY AND JOHN SEARLE'S DISKS, THE TOWNSEND BROWN / PAUL BIEFELD EFFECT, WRIGHT-PATTERSON ELECTRO-GRAVITICS SYS-TEMS, THE SECRETS OF AREA 51, QUANTUM PHYSICS AND PLASMA EXPERIMENTS. Articles on craft diagram, electro-gravitic propulsion, John Searle and his flying disks, eddie current propulsion, electromagnetic propulsion, superconducting plasma, electromagnetic reaction, UFOs and the Biefeld/Brown effect, background on Townsend Brown. notes from a patent on electrostatic propulsion, Brown's early patent specifications, charge fluctuations, origins, a 1956 document

taken from the technical library at Wright-Patterson AFB. It includes information on electro-gravitics, electrostatic energy, Townsend Brown, coupled condensers, VTOL vehicles, Dirac's theory, General Electric, thermo-nuclear electro-gravitics, literature on black budget aircraft. Articles include new propulsion and airframe designs, wedge-shaped craft, Aurora, mystery plane, hypersonic drones, XB-70, land seizures, black programs, donuts-on-a-rope, secret saucer base expeditions, unusually fanatical observers (UFOs), detectors, relativity II, quantum fluctuations, post-relativistics, Deutsche Physik, casimir potentials, spherical electromagnetics, quantum zeno, plasma transducer, and more. GRAV-03 • 148 pages • 8 1/2 x 11 • stapled binding • $23.00

GRAVITATION AND TACHYON FIELDS, THEORETICAL GRAVITATIONAL EXPLANATIONS, DETECTION OF RADIATION AND GRAVITY WAVES, GRAVITATIONAL INTERACTION AND RADIATION, OPTIMUM DESIGN OF GRAVITATIONAL ANTENNAS. Articles on concentric gravitation, tachyon fields, pressure/energy density, super-gravity, origin of gravity, pushing gravity, gravity waves, pressure zone, gravity induced resonant gravity-fields, mass sensors, gravity-wave astronomy, gravity-wave sources, interstellar gravitation radiation, Eotvos experiment, laser transducer, gravitational antennas and radiators, hydromagnetic and fundamental particles, measuring speed of gravitational interaction, notes from Robert L. Forward, finite velocity of gravitational fields, dynamic gravitational fields, designing a gravitational antenna for maximum gain, field patterns, frequency limitations, equations, and more. GRAV-04 • 209 pages • 8 1/2 x 11 • stapled binding • $32.00

TIME TRAVEL AND THE PHILADELPHIA EXPERIMENT, TIME AND THE GENERAL THEORY OF RELATIVITY, GRAVITATIONAL RADIATION IN SPACE-TIME, ELECTRO-DYNAMIC EQUATIONS OF MOTIONS, GRAVITATIONAL CONTROL RESEARCH. Articles on atomic clocks, time machines, truth beyond the Philadelphia experiment, invisible ships, teleportation, alternative explanations, invisibility techniques, the clock paradox in free fall, accelerating frames of reference, planetary astronomy, declassified document by the University of Detroit for the Armed Services Technical Information Agency from 1960-61. Topics include detection of gravity radiation, flat space-time relativity, rotational decay, electrodynamic equations, radiative reaction, Lorentz, Dirac, equations of motion, declassified master's thesis for the Arms Services Technical Information Agency in 1961. Topics include Townsend Brown, control over gravity, characteristics of gravitation, research effort, chronology, and more. GRAV-05 • 204 pages • 8 1/2 x 11 • stapled binding • $31.00

BACKGROUND INFORMATION ON ANTI-GRAVITY TECHNOLOGY—VOLUME ONE, Compiled by Tedd St. Rain. One each of the preceding 5 chapters (GRAV-01 through GRAV-05) combined into one book and made available at a special price. GRAV-91 • 888 pages • illustrated • 8 1/2 x 11 • stapled binding • $115.00

BACKGROUND INFORMATION ON ANTI-GRAVITY TECHNOLOGY—VOLUME TWO, Compiled by Tedd St. Rain. More gravity research including chapters on the role of gravitation in physics, Affine theory, effects on astronauts, speed of gravitation interaction, relativity for the experimentalist, mass detector for distant objects, guidelines to anti-gravity, zero-thrust velocity, ultracold neutrons, gravitational sensor, magnetic gradient sensors, value of ultracold neutrons, rotating inertial sensors, dynamic gravity detectors, rotating Newtonian fields, wide-band gravity antenna, gravitational gradiometer, wide-band antennas), estimated gravity, gravity from a quadruple, quantum mechanical particles, scalar and tensor radiation, terrain mapping gradiometer, estimates of gravitational radiation, and more. Note: GRAV-06 through GRAV-10 (not listed) combined into one book and made available at a special price. GRAV-92 • 958 pages • illustrated • 8 1/2 x 11 • stapled binding • $124.00

MAN MADE UFOS AND UNDERGROUND BASES. Articles on electrogravitic craft, Nazi UFOs, patents from various inventors, no UFOs, just secrets, Washington DC 1952 UFO flap, the AVRO, Holloman AFB sighting, UFOs, serious USAF business, Project Horizon, Russian anti-gravity plane, a lengthy proposal for a US Army Lunar Outpost, Project Horizon, General Twining's report on UFO intelligence, info on underground bases, and more. GRAV-11 • 130 pages • illustrated • 8 1/2 x 11 • stapled binding • $20.00

ELECTROGRAVITICS SYSTEMS: REPORTS ON A NEW PROPULSION METHODOLOGY. A reprint from the February 1956 report by the Gravity Research Group on the use of Townsend Brown patents and technologies to achieve electrogravitic flight control. Includes introductory notes, aviation report extracts, electrostatic patents, appendix of Townsend Brown patents, a summary of Townsend Brown's original patent specifications, the existence of negative mass, negative mass as a gravitational source of energy, and addition to articles on Area 51, Lazar, and other related topics. GRAV-12 • 122 pages • illustrated • 8 1/2 x 11 • stapled binding • $19.00

MIND CONTROL AND ELECTROMAGNETIC MANIPULATION

MIND CONTROL AND ELF MANIPULATION, MIND CONTROL AND MICROWAVE HARASSMENT, MIND CONTROL AND THE CIA, MIND CONTROL AND THE MILITARY. Articles on ELFs, wave manipulation, EEG entrainment, psychotronic warfare, microwaves, the woodpecker, mind control, microwaves, electronic surveillance, directed-energy weapons, covert harassment, psychotropic drugs, medical implants, star wars, NWO, CIA brainwashing techniques, terminal human behavior control, communist brainwashing, medical abuse, William Casey, the new mental battlefield, NIKE missile base, mind fields, electronic brain control, art of mesmerism, Indian rope trick, posthypnotic amnesia, and more. MIND-01 • 131 pages • illustrated • 8 1/2 x 11 • stapled binding • $20.00

MIND CONTROL AND PROJECT MK-ULTRA, MIND CONTROL AND PROJECT BLUEBIRD, BEWARE OF THE MIND CONTROLLERS. Documents include proceedings of the select committee on intelligence before the US Senate attempting to justify the CIA's program of research in behavioral modification. With testimony by ex-CIA and MK-ULTRA participants and their use of CBW, LSD, and other forms of inducement during the project. declassified and retrieved from microfilm, this document details the use of mind control drugs by the CIA in the 1950's. Topics include the OSI, hypnosis, psychiatry, psychology, lobotomies, various gases, hypnotic techniques, beating the polygraph, electroshock, LSD, MK-ULTRA, the use of "UFOs for psychological warfare" (according to a declassified CIA document), work by Martin Canon, hypnosis, US Navy brain-training, the 65 faces of Madonna, hidden television commercials, the TV junkies, and more. MIND-02 • 171 pages • 8 1/2 x 11 • stapled binding • $26.00

CONTROLLED OFFENSIVE BEHAVIOR—USSR. A declassified Defense Intelligence Agency document on Russian mind control. Topics include human behavior manipulations, soviet response, military psychology, psychological weapons, ESP, psychokinesis, hypnosis in medicine, artificial reincarnation, subliminals, sensory deprivation, pharmacology, and more. MIND-03 • 150 pages • 8 1/2 x 11 • stapled binding • $23.00

ELECTROMAGNETIC AND ACOUSTIC WEAPONRY, THE STRATEGIC DEFENSE INITIATIVE AND CROP CIRCLES Articles on Russian work on acoustics, high-tech crime fighting, EM pulse weapons, the mysterious Taos ELF sound, non-linear EMAG weapons, gravitational LASERs, invisible warfare, kinetic energy weapons, weather warfare, the EMAG spectrum, earthquakes and ELFs, beached whales, SDI, crop circles, Tesla coils, Tesla's long-range weapon, Tesla's secrets, anomalous crop circle data indicating the use of high-energy particle beam weaponry and more. MIND-04 • 88 pages • illustrated • 8 1/2 x 11 • stapled binding • $14.00

AN OVERVIEW OF MIND CONTROL AND ELECTROMAGNETIC MANIPULATION, compiled by Tedd St. Rain. One each of the preceding 4 chapters (MIND-01 through MIND-04) combined into one book and made available at a special price. MIND-91 • 613 pages • illustrated • 8 1/2 x 11 • stapled binding • $79.00

DOCUMENTATION OF REMOTE AND PHYSICAL MIND CONTROL AND BEHAVIOR MODIFICATION. This volume contains documentation on mind control and behavior modification. Includes articles on hypnosis, side tone delay, electron-narcosis, ultrasonics, Artichoke, lobotomies, Project Bluebird, QKHILLTOP, the disposal problem, LSD, MK Ultra, the CIA, programmed assassin, electromagnetic fields, flickering lights, psychotronic techniques, CIA finds way to mass-produce LSD, audio-visual brain entrainment, the perfect blackjack, MKULTRA Sub-project 55, "K" (knockout) research, MKULTRA Sub-project 61, implanted thermistors, Ewen Cameron, psychic driving, MKULTA Sub-project 75, psychotomimetic drugs, religious cults, guided animals, drug and chemical studies, bio-electronics, activation of human behavior by remote means, neurochemistry, MKDELTA, Richard Helms, chemical and biological warfare programs at Ft Detrick, MKSEARCH, MKNAOMI, the ORD files, and much more. MIND-05 • 129 pages • illustrated • 8 1/2 x 11 • stapled binding • $20.00

MIND CONTROL TECHNOLOGY PATENTS. Includes facsimiles of patents granted by the US Patent Office for the purposes of mental monitoring and mind alteration. Patents include a hearing device, apparatus and method for remotely monitoring and altering brain waves, method of and apparatus for inducing desired states of consciousness, method of inducing mental emotional and physical states of consciousness including specific mental activity in human beings. MIND-06 • 124 pages • illustrated • 8 1/2 x 11 • stapled binding • $19.00

MIND CONTROL AND BEHAVIOR MODIFICATION PATENTS. Includes facsimiles of patents granted by the US Patent Office for a hearing system (microwave), silent subliminal presentation system, system and method for controlling the nervous system of a living organism, multichannel system for and a multifractional method of controlling the nervous system of a living organism, brain wave inducing apparatus, method for obtaining neurophysiological effects, method and apparatus of brain wave form examination, method and apparatus for remotely determining information as to persons emotional state, method of changing a persons behavior, method of and apparatus for testing and indicating relaxation state of human subject, hearing device, apparatus for inducing frequency reduction in brain wave, individual identification and diagnosis using wave polarization, method for stimulation the falling asleep and/or relaxing behavior of a person and an arrangement therefore, device for the induction of specific brain wave patterns, method of inducing and maintaining various stages of sleep in the human being, apparatus for the treatment of neuropsychic and somatic disease with heat, light, sound and VHF electromagnetic radiation and much more. MIND-07 • 236 pages • illustrated • 8 1/2 x 11 • stapled binding • $36.00

ADDITIONAL MIND CONTROL RESEARCH DOCUMENTATION. The second in a series of mind control and behavior modification. Includes declassified Army documents, Senate hearings, Jose Delgado's bull experiments, NCRP report, biochips, the McMartin preschool incident, psychotronic warfare, and much more. MIND-08 • 117 pages • illustrated • 8 1/2 x 11 • stapled binding • $18.00

AN OVERVIEW OF MIND CONTROL AND PSYCHOLOGICAL WARFARE DOCUMENTATION, compiled by Tedd St. Rain. One each of the preceding 4 chapters (MIND-05 through MIND-08) combined into one book and made available at a special price. MIND-92 • 604 pages • illustrated • 8 1/2 x 11 • stapled binding • $78.00

PSYCHOLOGICAL OPERATIONS AND PSYCHOLOGI-CAL WARFARE. Articles on psychological weapons, the U.N., mind control by the media, Sirhan Sirhan letter and affidavit, psychiatric mind altering drugs, guns and doses, ritalin, psychiatric education, classroom shootings, and many others on the continuing programmed mayhem. MIND-09 • 216 pages • illustrated • 8 1/2 x 11 • stapled binding • $33.00

MIND CONTROL NEWSPAPER AND MAGAZINE ARTICLES. Topics include pentagon quest, influence of low intensity microwave on nervous function, mind-reading computer, big brother's tools are ready, ray gun is novel weapon, inventor hides secret of death ray, covert operations of the U.S. NSA, machines to read you mind, science fiction comes true, mind-reading project reveals secret, human perception of illumination with UHF electromagnetic energy, advances in neuroscience may threaten human rights, CIA able to control mind by hypnosis data shows, a fearful fix grips figure, a question of madness, pentagon unveils plans for a new crowd dispersal weapon, DoD looks at Russian mind control technology, mind control is a terrible thing to waste, spy budget made public by mistake, drug test by CIA, researchers get a peak at the brain's thought process, 14-year CIA project on controlling human behavior, pentagon to curtail electromagnetic tests, matador with radio stops bull, phaser on stun, exotic weaponry checked, an overview of a government mind control program, less-than-lethal weapons, voices lead to tragedy for two men, gunman's bizarre claims, big brother's coming, non-lethal weapons, ex-con plans class action suit again mind control, criminals can be brainwashed now, the mind's eye, effect of microwave radiation on birds, non-thermal effects, bill on leaks to media, mind control on the way scientist warns, new Tesla device like bolts of Thor, a new class of weapons and more. MIND-10 • 144 pages • illustrated • 8 1/2 x 11 • stapled binding • $22.00

ELECTROMAGNETIC TECHNOLOGY AND MIND CONTROL. Articles on mind wars, the zapping of America, cross currents, the guinea pigs, the sorcerer's challenge, non-lethal defense conference synopsis, federal regulation of medical devices, less-than-lethal weapons project, freedom of the mind as an international human rights issue, the development of new anti-personnel weapons, the soft kill fallacy, excerpt of CIA plan. CIA funds project at hospital, Mankind Research Unlimited Inc., symbiotic technology and education, bang you're alive, a subliminal Dr. Strangelove, pulsing magnets offer new method of mapping brain, lecturers worried by secret research projects, Hong Kong professor sues U.S. for mind control, microwave harassment and mind control experimentation, a letter from a victim, bombing suspects lose bid for secret files, mind controlled slave, electronic computer harassment, woman kills clerk at FCC headquarters, ailing mother who killed girl seeks release, accused murderer says he's the victim, suspect in Pentagon killing is found unfit to stand trial, allegation of behavior modification program using electronic surveillance, such things are known, woman fears government zapping, humans used as guinea pigs, non-lethal weapons, new world vistas, architectural electromagnetic shielding handbook, military use of space, low-intensity conflict and modern technology, the revolution in military affairs and conflict short of war, mind control testimony, electromagnetic pollution, CIA memorandum on controlling human behavior, the Smithsonian secret, mind reach, sites unseen and more. MIND-11 • 180 pages • illustrated • 8 1/2 x 11 • stapled binding • $27.00

ELECTROMAGNETIC MIND CONTROL TECHNOLOGY. Includes articles and documentation on the 'problem' defined, scientists and authors who have discussed this topic, classified program after cointelpro, the technology described, timeline of significant events, ideological problems, proof of EMF and mind control technology ignored, government cover-up in EMF policy, institutional problems, classified military research at universities, CIA stops non-conformity with its policy, interest groups control research and public information, military-industrial conference, bureaucratic problems, deeply entrenched classification system, illegal government experiments, electoral problems, general public unaware, information overload and suppression of information, economic problems, victims vs. US government, HAARP, advocacy groups, civil and political rights in the United States, working on the solution, planning for the miracle. MIND-12 • 200 pages • illustrated • 8 1/2 x 11 • stapled binding • $30.00

AN OVERVIEW OF ELECTROMAGNETIC MIND CONTROL TECHNOLOGY AND RESEARCH DOCUMENTATION, compiled by Tedd St. Rain. One each of the preceding 4 chapters (MIND-09 through MIND-12) combined into one book and made available at a special price. MIND-93 • 740 pages • illustrated • 8 1/2 x 11 • stapled binding • $96.00

WEATHER MODIFICATION, CONTROL AND HAARP. MIND-13 • 110 pages • illustrated • 8 1/2 x 11 • stapled binding • $17.00

MILITARY OPERATIONS OTHER THAN WAR (OOTW), IMPLANTABLE BIOTELEMETRY SYSTEMS AND PHYSICAL CONTROL OF THE MIND. MIND-14 • 138 pages • illustrated • 8 1/2 x 11 • stapled binding • $21.00

IEEE TRANSACTIONS ON MICROWAVE THEORY AND TECHNIQUES, 1971, 1973, 1974, 1977. Articles include the tri-service program, interaction of microwave and radio frequency radiation with biological systems, biological function as influenced by low-power modulated RF energy, microwave radiation safety standards in eastern Europe, absence of heart-rate effects in rabbits during low-level microwave irradiation, evidence for non-thermal effects of microwave radiation, quantifying hazardous electromagnetic fields, induced fields and heating within a cranial structure irradiated by an electromagnetic plane wave, new techniques for implementing microwave biological exposure systems, electromagnetic fields and relative heating patterns due to a rectangular aperture source in direct contact with bi-layered biological tissue, microwave heating of simulated human limbs by aperture sources, determination and elimination of hazardous microwave fields aboard Naval ships, selective electromagnetic

heating of tumors in animals in deep hypothermia, prolongation of life during high-intensity microwave exposures, microwave of the 1970s, 1973 international microwave symposium, power deposition in a spherical model of man exposed to 1 to 20 megahertz of electromagnetic fields, characterizations of non-linearities in microwave devices and systems, general acoustic signals by pulsed microwave energy, on microwave-induced hearing sensation, rank reduction of ill-conditioned matrices in wave-guide junction problems, further studies on the microwave auditory effect, theoretical analysis of acoustical signal generation in materials irradiated with microwave energy and more. MIND-15 • 195 pages • illustrated • 8 1/2 x 11 • stapled binding • $30.00

EMERGENCY POWERS, NON-LETHAL AND RADIO FREQUENCY WEAPONS, ELECTRONIC SURVEILLANCE, AND RESEARCH ARTICLES. MIND-16 • 91 pages • 8 1/2 x 11 • stapled binding • $14.00

ALIEN ABDUCTION AS ARCHETYPE OR PSYCHOLOGICAL OPERATIONS. Articles on extraterrestrial nightmares, mass programming, alien invasion propaganda, project open book, anatomy of an abduction, the search for signals from space, that alien feeling, holographic universe, Rockefeller/UFO connection, J. Dewey, UFO briefing document, Carnegie Endowment for International Peace, unmasking the disinformers, demons, doctors and aliens, CIA/UFO links, Linda Napolitano, and more. MIND-17 • 163 pages • illustrated • 8 1/2 x 11 • stapled binding • $25.00

AN OVERVIEW OF WEATHER, OPTIONS OTHER THAN WAR, MICROWAVE THEORY, BIOTELEMETRY, RF WEAPONS AND ALIEN ABDUCTION, compiled by Tedd St. Rain. One each of the preceding 5 chapters (MIND-13 through MIND-17) combined into one book and made available at a special price. MIND-94 • 697 pages • illustrated • 8 1/2 x 11 • stapled binding • $90.00

HEALTH AND HEALING ISSUES

FOOD, FLUORIDE, and MERCURY POISONING, MALATHION AND PESTICIDE POLLUTION, CHEMICAL AND BIOLOGICAL WARFARE. Articles on fluoride's link to bone cancer, mercury amalgams and antibiotic resistance, new carpets and illness, drug residues in milk, food irradiation, male impotence, agent orange, pesticides, malathion, the medfly, toxic waste, Nazi development of nerve agents and pesticides, maternal exposure, sensitivities, chemical legacy, cholinesterase poisoning, CBW and universities, Army testing on civilians, the Dengue epidemic, CIA-FBI ties, UCSF testing, Congressional appropriations, flesh-eating bacteria, and more. CBW-01 • 171 pages • illustrated • 8 1/2 x 11 • stapled binding • $26.00

THE AIDS PANDEMIC FROM CAIB, AIDS AND POPULATION CONTROL, HIV-NEGATIVE NON-CONTAGIOUS AIDS. Articles from CovertAction Intelligence Bulletin on the AIDS epidemic. Includes six theories of origin, genetic engineering, population control, dioxin, Dengue, Maguari, CBW, African swine flu, co-factors, smallpox vaccine, Fort Detrick, resource list, the Congressional appropriations for an AIDS-like biological agent, an AIDS contract, designer diseases, genetic engineering, polio, skull valley, other methods of population control, HIV-negative AIDS including AIDS link to chemicals, the Iatrogenic connection, acquisition from drugs, the American connection, immunizations, Peter Duesberg reprint, and more. CBW-02 • 177 pages • illustrated • 8 1/2 x 11 • stapled binding • $27.00

REPORTS ON WORLD DEPOPULATION, ALTERNATIVE MEDICINE AND AIDS, THE PHARMACEUTICAL AND MEDICAL CARTELS. Articles on Haig-Kissinger depopulation policy, how Kissinger, Bush and Scowcroft plotted Third World genocide, the agendas of the UN, the IMF, the World Bank, Global 2000, neutralizing AIDS with vitamins, using ozone, Bob Beck neutralizer, alternative therapies, resource guides, FDA raids, licensing, fighting for your rights, the war on supplements, HR 3642, pharmaceutical companies, health cartels and more. CBW-03 • 138 pages • 8 1/2 x 11 • stapled binding • $21.00

A PROFILE OF CHEMICAL AND BIOLOGICAL WARFARE METHODS, compiled by Tedd St. Rain. One each of the preceding 3 chapters (CBW-01 through CBW-03) combined into one book and made available at a special price. CBW-91 • 486 pages • illustrated • 8 1/2 x 11 • stapled binding • $63.00

HIV AND AIDS DOCUMENTATION. Articles on 50 USC 1520, release of germ warfare in Capital, experiments on civilian populations, AIDS references, chronology of AIDS in America, Chemical and Biological Warfare House Hearings 1970, viruses as pesticides, germ warfare accident, what the government doesn't tell you about AIDS, saliva and HIV, killer condoms, herd immunity and the HIV epidemic, multi-drug resistant TB, resistance of AIDS virus at room temperature, HIV agent summary statement, CDC response to crisis, house of commons report on problems associated with AIDS, and more. CBW-04 • 139 pages • illustrated • 8 1/2 x 11 • stapled binding • $21.00

HIV AND AIDS IN PRINT. Articles from a variety of sources including the wire services, major newspapers, magazines, and journals. Topics include news from the early 90s, how HIV, works, AIDS contracted through soccer injury, South African AIDS, HIV remains active, Smallpox vaccine, hybrid AIDS, AIDS and the dentist, AIDS vs Ebola, the AIDS Hotel, candidiasis, modern Galileos, WHO's influence, replication of the AIDS virus, measles incident rate, Bovine leukemia virus, Robert Gallo, Fort Detrick, viral oncology, leukemia and sarcoma, special virus cancer program 1971, grants, annual funding, monkey inoculation and more. CBW-05 • 137 pages • illustrated • 8 1/2 x 11 • stapled binding • $21.00

THE ORIGIN OF AIDS, ARTICLES AND REPORTS ON THE SUBJECT. Articles on diet versus AIDS, the origin of AIDS, the epidemic of lies, is African swine flu fever the cause, HTLV-3, healing AIDS naturally, AIDS inc., the AIDS/nuclear fallout connection, understanding AIDS, AIDS and hepatitis, updates on AIDS and blood, AIDS link to smallpox vaccine, Cocaine spurs AIDS, epidemic of AIDS in Africa, science by name calling, misconduct in AIDS discovery by Gallo, AIDS and immunity, a different kind of plague, stress and your immune system, the untreated live longer, doctor's strike - death rate falls, the heretic, Peter Duesberg interview, complexity of AIDS, weapons against AIDS, double danger of AIDS, AIDS and civil rights, theoretical background for treatment, surviving AIDS, dueling hypotheses, rethinking AIDS, the HIV gap, AIDS epidemiology, AIDS acquired by drug consumption and other non-contagious risk factors, disputed test and more. CBW-06 • 148 pages • illustrated • 8 1/2 x 11 • stapled binding • $23.00

GULF WAR ILLNESS AND ITS CAUSES AND SECRECY. This package explores the alarming escalation of death and illnesses related to Dessert Shield / Desert Storm and what can be done about it. Includes articles on vaccination waivers, Secretary of Defense memorandum, cover-up of Gulf War Syndrome, U.S. Senate report on sales of biologicals/chemicals to Iraq, et al, military research, chronic fatigue illnesses and Gulf War syndrome, info on Cipro, Biaxin, Doxycycline, etc, Libya, secrecy, storage locations, and much more. CBW-07 • 105 pages • illustrated • 8 1/2 x 11 • stapled binding • $16.00

AN OVERVIEW OF HIV AND AIDS, ORIGINS OF AIDS, AND THE GULF WAR ILLNESS, compiled by Tedd St. Rain. One each of the preceding 4 chapters (CBW-04 through CBW-07) combined into one book and made available at a special price. CBW-92 • 530 pages • illustrated • 8 1/2 x 11 • stapled binding • $69.00

CHEMICAL AGENT AND WEAPONS RESEARCH. This gem of a report, released under the FOIA, details the Use of Volunteers in Chemical Agent Research. It begins with a series of correspondence between the department of the Army and the Surgeon General which covers private citizens, claims against the government, life insurance, legality of accepting volunteers. The report then continues with a history of chemical warfare, psychochemicals, LSD, perception of the threat, human volunteer selection, informed consent, chemical warfare experimentation with humans at Edgewood Arsenal, field testing in Fort Bragg, Fort McClellan, Fort Benning, and Dugway Proving Ground, Intelligence Corps LSD testing, third chance, derby hat, contracts with civilian institutions, research costs and a bibliography. CBW-08 • 179 pages • illustrated • 8 1/2 x 11 • stapled binding • $27.00

BIOLOGICAL AND BEHAVIORAL MODIFICATION TESTING INVOLVING HUMAN SUBJECTS BY THE DEPARTMENT OF DEFENSE. The complete project MK-ULTRA senate report, and additional documentation, details over 30 years of experiments conducted by the Department of Defense on the American people without their knowledge or consent. This shocking document reveals the numerous government test of biological weapons in places like New York, where biologicals were released in the subway systems, Pennsylvania, where tunnels were filled with live organisms, as well as spraying off the coast of California to see how far inland disease would spread. CBW-09 • 175 pages • illustrated • 8 1/2 x 11 • stapled binding • $27.00

HUMAN DRUG TESTING BY THE C.I.A. More evidence of the government's involvement in human experimentation for the purpose of controlling people and their actions. Proceedings from Senate hearings on the subject, and more. CBW-10 • 269 pages • illustrated • 8 1/2 x 11 • stapled binding • $41.00

AN OVERVIEW OF CHEMICAL, BIOLOGICAL AND BEHAVIORAL MODIFICATIONS, AND HUMAN DRUG TESTING, compiled by Tedd St. Rain. One each of the preceding 3 chapters (CBW-08 through CBW-10) combined into one book and made available at a special price. CBW-93 • 623 pages • illustrated • 8 1/2 x 11 • stapled binding • $81.00

DON'T GET THAT VACCINE: DOCUMENTATION ON THE DANGER OF VACCINES, IMMUNIZATIONS, BOOSTER AND FLU SHOTS. Topics include anti-vaccinists, immunization a deadly farce, mandatory vaccinations, CDR MMWR, immunizing children, vaccination dangers, baby shots, state law changes, medical time bomb, HHS lawsuit, Lederle Acellular vaccine, CDC eliminated DPT contraindications, WHO killed Africa, Pertussis vaccine can cause brain damage, dangers of immunization, baby spits up vaccine - gives dad polio, is HIV the cause of AIDS, hour of time transcript, the germ theory, Enderlein therapy, ozone therapy, milk pasteurization, court transcripts, different reactions, excerpts from the book The Wonderful Century by Alfred Russel Wallace 1899 and morex. CBW-11 • 252 pages • illustrated • 8 1/2 x 11 • stapled binding • $38.00

THE ROYAL R. RIFE REPORT, NEW MICROSCOPES, CORRESPONDENCE, PHOTOS, AND VACCINATION AS AN ILLUSION. COLLOIDAL SILVER, ELECTRO MEDICINE, BOB BECK'S RESEARCH, AND MORE. The Royal Raymond Rife was best known for the invention of a microscope in the 1930s that could detect very small bacteria and even viruses. Once he was able to see the pathogen in question he started experimenting with electromagnetic frequency bombardment and developed data on which pathogens were affected, and killed, by which frequencies. At first he had the backing of medical science and the FDA, but when the technology was shown to be effective at very little cost to the patient the powers-that-be shut his research down, the laboratory mysterious burned down, and he ended up dying in a federal prison as a result. A must read for people not familiar with his work. Also includes the history of colloidal silver, blue bloods, the plague, banishing disease, building your own colloidal silver generator, Bob Beck's research, biological warfare and more. CBW-12 • 172 pages • illustrated • 8 1/2 x 11 • stapled binding • $26.00

INFORMATION ON ACUPUNCTURE, ACUPRESSURE, IRIDIOLOGY, INCLUDING CHARTS, NOTES, AND RESEARCH MATERIAL. CBW-13 • 240 pages • illustrated • 8 1/2 x 11 • stapled binding • $36.00

AN OVERVIEW OF ROYAL R. RIFE, VACCINATION HAZARDS, ELECTROMEDICINE, ACUPUNCTURE, ACUPRESSURE AND MORE, compiled by Tedd St. Rain. One each of the preceding 3 chapters (CBW-11 through CBW-13) combined into one book and made available at a special price. CBW-94 • 664 pages • illustrated • 8 1/2 x 11 • stapled binding • $86.00

GEM THERAPY, SRI KANTA, NATURE AND POWER OF GEMS, GEMS AND COSMIC RAYS, FIVE ELEMENTS AND DIET, TELETHERAPY, DISEASES AND GEM PRESCRIPTIONS. Gem therapy is very popular in certain parts of Asia and in India. This compilation contains excerpts from books on the subject, notes from a class and additional excerpts from an out-of-print book called 'gem therapy.' Topics include the seven rays of the rainbow, nature and power of gems, gems and cosmic rays, gems and the rainbow, gems in ayurvedic, gems in astrology, gem therapy and applied science, disease and cosmic rays, the seven plexii and disease, gem teletherapy the subtle anatomy of man, gem medicines, gem prescriptions, and some case studies. CBW-14 • 235 pages • illustrated • 8 1/2 x 11 • stapled binding • $36.00

RATIONAL BACTERIOLOGY: ELEMENTS OF DRUGLESS THERAPIES FOR DISEASE 1933. Topics include bacteria in general, study bacteria, pathogenicity, infection, immunity, classifications, staphylococcus, streptococcus, pneumococcus, gram negative, coliform group, spore forming anaerobes, cholera, diphtheria, tubercle, animal parasites, filterable viruses, bacteriophage, cell division, crystallization, infection, pathology, the Biont cycle, etiology, hematopoiesis, platelets, neurology, inoculation, allergies, significance to chiropractors, bacteriology and the scientific method, theory of immunity, the theory of microzyma, and more. CBW-15 • 181 pages • illustrated • 8 1/2 x 11 • stapled binding • $28.00

GLOBAL MANIPULATION

SPIRIT OF '76: ROOTS OF FREEDOM, THE NOW: SURRENDERING OUR NATION, THE CENTRAL INTELLIGENCE AGENCY. Includes the Declaration of Independence, the Monroe doctrine, the Gettysburg Address, the Star Spangled Banner, The Constitution, giving up US sovereignty, includes the Marine questionnaire, concentration camps for US citizens, the UN, a world police force, MJTF, REX '84, foreign troops in US, CIA's role in spying, bombing, BCCI, Watergate, Dulles, Castro, Pan Am 103, and more. NWO-01 • 135 pages • illustrated • 8 1/2 x 11 • stapled binding • $21.00

MYSTERIOUS DEATH AND MURDER CONSPIRACIES, WACO OKC AND MILITIAS, FEMA VS YOUR CONSTITUTIONAL RIGHTS, THE NEW WORLD ORDER SPOTLIGHT EXPOSE. Articles on the mysterious deaths of Star Wars scientists at Marconi, USS Liberty-gate, Kemper Marley, Casolaro and INSLAW, Wackenhut annual reports, JFK, Waco, the Partin report on OKC, the Fed-Up intelligence summary, citizens militias, swat standoffs, from Salem to Waco, Waco search warrant, executive orders, computerization, Carter's legacy, US dictatorship, secret activities, the proper crisis, mount weather, undefined emergency, NSDD-47, the trilateral commission, elite planning, world government, NWO, US Dictatorship, Constitution suspended, Bilderbergs, Middle East, Central America, and more. NWO-02 • 221 pages • illustrated • 8 1/2 x 11 • stapled binding • $34.00

REVELATIONS OF AWARENESS: NEW WORLD ORDER, FASCISM ALIVE IN AMERICA TODAY, SMART CARDS TOWARDS A CASHLESS SOCIETY, IMPLANTABLE MICROCHIP TECHNOLOGIES. A new-age newsletter outlining the NWO. Topics include street gangs, one world religion, the UN, economic meltdown, microchip implants, gun control, the UN, an American police state, forfeiture laws, NSDDs, neo-fascism, global plantation, environmental regulations, America in Peril, public conditioning for smart cards, big brother, health cards, electronic transfers, the "MARC," redesigned currency, hand and fingerprint scanners, euro-dollars, barcodes, implantable biochips, eye-in-the-sky, Destron/IDI, AVID, InfoPet, Trovan, gun triggers, the beast, teeth wired for sound, implanted psychics, brain implants, misc. articles, and more. NWO-03 • 190 pages • illustrated • 8 1/2 x 11 • stapled binding • $29.00

HISTORICAL TIMELINES OF HUMAN HISTORY, THE SECRET HISTORY AND GENEALOGY OF THE NEW WORLD ORDER, BACKGROUND INFORMATION ON BUSH SR. AND CLINTON. A compilation of timelines from various sources, from 40,000 BC to 1985 AD. An interesting assortment of facts on the history of the human race. Also includes papers that detail the influence of the Rockefellers, freemasonry, Bush and Clinton, banking cartels, Bilderbergers, committee of 300, Phoenix project, genealogical charts, John Birchers, Perot, Jupiter Island, Prescott and Neil Bush, Harriman, Hitler and Nazism, opium smuggling, skull and bones, Zapata oil, CIA, JFK, and more. NWO-04 • 169 pages • 8 1/2 x 11 • stapled binding • $26.00

A NEW WORLD ORDER TOWARDS A ONE WORLD GOVERNMENT, Compiled by Tedd St. Rain. One each of the preceding 4 chapters (NWO-01 through NWO-04) combined into one book and made available at a special price. NWO-91 • 792 or 715 pages • illustrated • 8 1/2 x 11 • stapled binding • $102.00 or $93.00

THE COVERT INTELLIGENCE FILES. A compilation of documents which detail the ongoing government involvement in illicit activities. Topics include Clinton's association with Dan Lasater, Don Tyson and Drug Smuggling in Arkansas, the death of Vince Foster, a closer look at the Whitewater investigation, Larry Nichols, Paula Jones, and much more. Includes military intelliegence files. NWO-05 • 225 pages • illustrated • 8 1/2 x 11 • stapled binding • $34.00

DRUGS, LAW ENFORCEMENT AND FOREIGN POLICY: HEARINGS BEFORE THE SUBCOMMITTEE ON TERRORISM, NARCOTICS AND INTERNATIONAL COMMUNICATIONS OF THE COMMITTEE ON FOREIGN RELATIONS, UNITED STATES SENATE. As the name implies these are the proceedings discussing Drugs and Terrorism, presided over by the Hon. John F. Kerry, chairman of the subcommittee. The "Kerry Hearings," as they have become known use 'hooded' witnesses (from the witness protection program), military generals, and a New York district attorney, amongst others, to blow the lid off of drug smuggling operations south of the border. It has long been know of CIA's involvement in these covert operations but this congressional testimony is another smoking gun as to Gen. Noriega and Bill Casey's participation. NWO-06 • 192 pages • 8 1/2 x 11 • stapled binding • $29.00

CIA DRUG SMUGGLING AND FORFEITURE LAWS, THE PHONY WAR AGAINST DRUGS, U.S. GOVERNMENT IMPORTATION AND DISTRIBUTION OF DRUGS. A comprehensive collection on the government's ongoing involvement in the world-wide drug trade, profits from which fund many clandestine and/or black budget projects. Articles include the CIA and the war on drugs, LSD, laundering, S&Ls, Iran-Contra, property seizure, civil forfeiture, informants, legalization, FIJA, drug cartels, drug raids, dope squads, Asian heroin, extensive documentation on the Mena connection, Terry Reed, Bill Clinton, the big white lie, the CIA and crack cocaine, Michael Ruppert ongoing work, court documents, Senate hearings, the doping of America, John Kerry hearings, opium and national security. NWO-07 • 304 pages • 8 1/2 x 11 • stapled binding • $46.00

AN OVERVIEW OF THE INTELLIGENCE FILES, CONCENTRATION CAMPS AND THE DRUG WAR, Compiled by Tedd St. Rain. One each of the preceding 3 chapters (NWO-05 through NWO-07) combined into one book and made available at a special price. NWO-92 • 721 pages • illustrated • 8 1/2 x 11 • stapled binding • $94.00

CONCENTRATION CAMPS IN AMERICA, CIVILIAN LABOR PROGRAM, FM 41-10 EXCERPTS, OPERATION GARDEN PLOT, PABST DOCUMENT. Learn about the Army's Draft Regulations on their "Civilian Labor Program." Designed primarily for civilian inmates, there is much speculation on the purpose of prison-like facilities sitting empty (for the time being) nationwide. The next document is an excerpt from FM 41-10, the Civil Affairs Operations Manual from the U.S. Army. Up next is the U.S. Air Force's "civil disturbance plan" codenamed "Garden Plot," is a classic from the 1980s on how the Air Force would use its personnel in the event of civil unrest in this country. Finally, another classic from 1979 called "Concentration Camp Plans for U.S. Citizens. NWO-08 • 245 pages • 8 1/2 x 11 • stapled binding • $37.00

THE UNITED NATIONS AND GLOBAL GOVERNMENT. Includes text from U.S. Senate resolutions relative to the United Nations charter from 1950, Hegelian Principle, global government, War Powers act, Isolationism, North Atlantic treaty, collective security with the U.N., disarmament, U.N. Headquarters agreement 1947, Foreign Affairs list for U.N., 16th Amendment violated, treaties vs. The Constitution, Foreign Affairs: The Hard Road to World Order, House hearing on The World Trade Organization, the United States program for general and complete disarmament in a peaceful world, charter of the U.N. and more. NWO-09 • 151 pages • 8 1/2 x 11 • stapled binding • $23.00

THE POLITICS OF CHANGE IN LOCAL GOVERNMENT REFORM. An fascinating Resolution (No. 447-74) of the Board of Supervisors of the County of El Dorado, California concerning the restructuring of local government in the event of a government's "collapse," a "crisis" or some other such "catastrophe" as to render the present government invalid. The Summary of Conclusions in this report states "There must be a CLIMATE FOR CHANGE in order for the restructuring of local government to occur, whether this restructuring involves drastic reform, reorganization, modernization, or a minor administrative alignment." No doubt resolutions such as this have been 'passed' nationwide. NWO-10 • 114 pages • 8 1/2 x 11 • stapled binding • $18.00

THE JFK-TIPPIT CONNECTION AND THE TWO OSWALDS. Lee Harvey Oswald was arrested in a Texas theater for the murder of police officer J. D. Tippit on November 22, 1963. Officer Tippit, who bore a striking resemblance to President Kennedy, was murdered within 45 minutes of the shooting of the president, and less than 4 miles away. Eyewitness reports of the dead president after the autopsy, including Jackie's, indicated that Kennedy "did not look like himself." Is there a connection? This report investigates the coincidences between the murders of these two men, includes autopsy and medical reports of Kennedy, Tippit and Oswald. Interesting reading for those so inclined. NWO-11 • 82 pages • 8 1/2 x 11 • stapled binding • $13.00

AN OVERVIEW OF CONCENTRATION CAMPS, THE U.N. AND GLOBAL GOVERNMENT, POLITICS OF CHANGE, and JFK-TIPPIT CONNECTION compiled by Tedd St. Rain. One each of the preceding 4 chapters (NWO-08 through NWO-11) combined into one book and made available at a special price. NWO-93 • 592 pages • illustrated • 8 1/2 x 11 • stapled binding • $77.00

GUN CONTROL, THE NRA, STATE PRE-EMPTION, AND THE L.E.A.A. For the past two decades the National Rifle Association has been bastion of gun-owner's rights in America. However, they've stood by while state-after-state have based "pre-emption" laws, in effect regulating personal firearms on the state level, and in many cases placing extremely restrictive bans on all types of firearms. This package provides ongoing documentation of this issue with articles on firearms pre-emption laws, a national strategy to reduce crime, handguns, NRA soft on guns, the Law Enforcement Assistance Administration (L.E.A.A.), omnibus crime control and safe streets act, federal pre-emption of state and local authority, NRA anti-gun vote, and more. NWO-12 • 170 pages • 8 1/2 x 11 • stapled binding • $26.00

THE COUNCIL ON FOREIGN RELATIONS: 1998-99 ANNUAL REPORT. Learn about today's CFR, as it becomes a "more national and more diverse" organization. This fancy report reveals more by what it doesn't say. Includes the role of the CFR, studies program, meetings program, Washington program (remember it's based in NYC), national program, corporate program, publishing endeavors, committee lists of the board, by-laws of the council, budget and finance, staff, membership selection and roster, and more. NWO-13 • 143 pages • 8 1/2 x 11 • stapled binding • $22.00

THE NEW WORLD ORDER, THE NEW AMERICA THE NEW WORLD, AND THE ANNALS OF BOHEMIAN GROVE. Few people are aware that in the 1930s the famous author H.G. Wells wrote a book called The New World Order. While considered tame compared to today's standards of what comprises the new world, his views on the "new revolution" and "class warfare" have become the standards we have come to live by. H.G. Wells had previously written another book called The New America, The New World in which he details his vision for where America is positioned in the forecast of our future. This volume concludes with an excerpt from "The Annals of the Bohemian Club: Volume VI, 1973-1987." Don't ask, don't tell. For those with an interest in such things, these 38 pages are dynamite. For those of you not in the "know," Bohemian Grove is an exclusive resort on a stand of ancient redwoods in California that hosts special events for the global elite and a two-week long conference in July where world leaders watch and sometimes take part in theatrical acts and plays some of which involve worshiping an owl deity, mock human sacrifices, cremation rituals, and other unusual activities. NWO-14 • 155 pages • 8 1/2 x 11 • stapled binding • $24.00

STATE OF ILLINOIS NATIONAL GUARD INTERNAL SECURITY PLAN: STATE MILITARY FORCES SUPPORT TO CIVIL AUTHORITITES. An example from Springfield, IL, of the plans in place nationwide for using the national guard and other military forces to quell civil disturbances. Includes definitions, civilian responsibility, military planning, laws governing the use of troops, advice and counsel for members of the national guard, public affairs, operations, logistics, communications, intelligence, fiscal implications, ammunition, civil disturbance conditions, and more. NWO-15 • 102 pages • 8 1/2 x 11 • stapled binding • $16.00

AN OVERVIEW OF GUN CONTROL, THE COUNCIL ON FOREIGN RELATIONS, THE NEW WORLD ORDER, BOHEMIAN GROVE, INTERNAL SECURITY PLAN AND MORE, compiled by Tedd St. Rain. One each of the preceding 4 chapters (NWO-12 through NWO-15) combined into one book and made available at a special price. NWO-94 • 570 pages • illustrated • 8 1/2 x 11 • stapled binding • $74.00

THE ANTICHRIST,THE U.N., THE N.W.O. AND THE CLUB OF ROME. NWO-16 • 109 pages • 8 1/2 x 11 • stapled binding • $17.00

BLUEPRINT FOR THE PEACE RACE: OUTLINE OF BASIC PROVISIONS OF A TREATY ON A GENERAL AND COMPLETE DISARMAMENT IN A PEACEFUL WORLD, U.S. ARMS CONTROL AND DISARMAMENT POLICY, GORBACHEV'S PERESTROIKA, FREEDOM FROM WAR. Articles on the basic outline of the proposed treaty, arms control and disarmament, in the cause of peace, worldwide anti-missile defense system, should the U.N. have an army?, the U.S. ACDA, post-cold war plan, perestroika, Russia, Iraq, U.N. Charter revisions 1950, 1953, visit of Gorbachev, U.N. operations, 21st-Century Asia, the Dis-United States, Brady Bill, freedom from war, declaration of disarmament and more. NWO-17 • 219 pages • 8 1/2 x 11 • stapled binding • $33.00

WORLD STATE'S SUPER SECRET CONSTITUTION, FEDERAL RESERVE RESOLUTIONS, THE U.N., THE LAWS OF WAR, DECLARATION OF AN AGRICULTURAL EMERGENCY, EMERGENCY POWERS, FOREIGN POLICY ARMS CONTROL AND DISARMAMENT. Includes reports on a highly restrictive secret document setting up a new world government which would supplant the U.N., abolish the U.S. and other countries as nations and govern, tax and regulate the world's people. Also articles on SCA-25, necessity to abolish, trading with the enemy, constitutional sources of the laws of war, federal reserve act commentary from 1933, our foreign policy, armed forces laws and more. NWO-18 • 271 pages • 8 1/2 x 11 • stapled binding • $41.00

NO TIME FOR SLAVES, DEBT MONEY, BILLIONS FOR THE BANKERS, CONSTITUTIONAL CONVENTION, AND MORE. NWO-19 • 100 pages • illustrated • 8 1/2 x 11 • stapled binding • $15.00

AN OVERVIEW OF THE U.N., THE CLUB OF ROME, BLUEPRINT FOR PEACE, LAWS OF WAR, AND BILLIONS FOR THE BANKERS, compiled by Tedd St. Rain. One each of the preceding 4 chapters (NWO-16 through NWO-19) combined into one book and made available at a special price. NWO-95 • 699 pages • illustrated • 8 1/2 x 11 • stapled binding • $91.00

THE MONETARY SYSTEM

TALES FROM THE TREASURY, BACKGROUND ON THE FEDERAL RESERVE SYSTEM, UNDERSTANDING THE UNIFORM COMMERICAL CODE, SOVEREIGN CITIZENSHIP. In the 1970's and 80's Byron C. Dale wrote a series of letters back and forth to the treasury department asking a series of questions about our money. Topics include the federal reserve, lawful money, cost per coin, cost per note, definition of a dollar, how is money created, treasury notes, t-bills, national gold banks, request for redemption of currency, and many more entertaining and informative exchanges. Also articles on the federal reserve, the Rothschilds, Warburgs, J.P. Morgan, board of governors, bankrupting America, brief history of the Federal Reserve, what went wrong, know your money (from the Fed), Swiss banks, Chase, currency makeover, the UCC connection, legal tyranny, jurisdiction, admiralty courts, remedy and recourse, zip codes, common law contract, the lawyer's secret oath, the 1867 constitution, 14th amendment, universal citizens, informed consent, government bankruptcy, what to do when they ask for your SSN, your SSN decoded, debtors and creditors, legal fraud, and more. SOV-01 • 192 pages • 8 1/2 x 11 • stapled binding 29.00

BACKGROUND ON THE INCOME TAX SYSTEM, DRIVING A VEHICLE IS A RIGHT NOT A PRIVILEGE, SUPPORTING EVIDENCE FROM CASE LAW CITATIONS. Articles on the early days, wealth taxes, diagrams, forms, tax reforms, travelling, driving, privileges, state proclamations, state permits, officer questionnaire, affidavit, cites, reference, case law, citizenship, Maxwell vs. Dow, 14th amendment, 5th amendment, natural rights, Twining vs. NJ, writ of habeas corpus, marriages, voter registration, allodial titles, non-citizens, employment taxes, and more. SOV-02 • 202 pages • 8 1/2 x 11 • stapled binding • $31.00

GUIDELINES TO OUR MONETARY SYSTEM AND SOVEREIGNTY, Compiled by Tedd St. Rain. One each of the preceding 2 chapters (SOV-01 through SOV-02) combined into one book and made available at a special price. SOV-91 • 479 pages • illustrated • 8 1/2 x 11 • stapled binding • $63.00

COMPLETE RESEARCH ARCHIVE, Compiled by Tedd St. Rain. One each of the preceding 70 chapters (EMAG-01 through SOV-03) combined into one book and made available at a special price. Inquire about recently acquired material not including in this total. COMPLETE-91 • 12336 pages • illustrated • 8 1/2 x 11 • stapled binding • $1233.00

To order individual items add $5.00 shipping and handling for the first item and $1.00 for each additional item. Send your check or money order to (CA residents add 8.25% sales tax): Lost Arts Media, Post Office Box 15026, Long Beach, CA 90815. For more information visit www.lostartsmedia.com or to order by credit card call 1 (800) 952-LOST or 1 (562) 596-ARTS.

All of the Following Books are 6 x 9 and Trade Paper
Check for Availability before Ordering 1 (800) 952-LOST

Stage Magic and Tricks

After-Dinner Sleights and Pocket Tricks, by C. Lang Neil. ISBN 1-59016-011-8 • 92 pages • illustrated • GB£7.95 • US$11.95

Book of Tricks and Magic: Containing a Choice Selection of Tricks and Games for Parlor Entertainment, edited by Professor Svengarro. ISBN 1-59016-079-7 • 88 + 12 pages • illustrated • GB£7.95 • US$11.95

Fifty New Card Tricks: A Comprehensive Description of the Continuous Front and Back Hand Palm with Cards, by Howard Thurston. ISBN 1-59016-239-0 • 83 + 12 pages • illustrated • GB£7.95 • US$11.95

Gilbert Coin Tricks for Boys and Girls, by Alfred C. Gilbert. ISBN 1-59016-283-8 • 60 + 42 pages • illustrated • GB£7.95 • US$11.95

Magic for Home and Stage, by the Shrewesbury Publishing Company. ISBN 1-59016-502-0 • 150 pages • illustrated • GB£9.95 • US$14.95

Modern Card Effects and How to Perform Them, by George DeLawrence and James "Kater" Thompson. ISBN 1-59016-523-3 • 80 + 12 pages • illustrated • GB£7.95 • US$11.95

Modern Card Tricks Without Apparatus, by Will Goldston. ISBN 1-59016-524-1 • 109 pages • illustrated • GB£7.95 • US$11.95

New Book of Coin Tricks, by Professor Svengarro. ISBN 1-59016-557-8 • 92 pages • illustrated • GB£7.95 • US$11.95

New Book of Parlor Tricks and Magic, by Hernandez. ISBN 1-59016-558-6 • 61 + 47 pages • illustrated • GB£8.95 • US$12.95

Parlor Book of Magic and Drawing Room Entertainments, edited by Signor Blitz. ISBN 1-59016-638-8 • 214 pages • illustrated • GB£12.95 • US$17.95

Professional Magic Tricks Revealed, by George Milburn. ISBN 1-59016-679-5 • 64 + 44 pages • illustrated • GB£7.95 • US$11.95

The Secrets of Houdini, by J. C. Cannell. ISBN 1-59016-759-7 • 279 pages • illustrated • GB£15.95 • US$20.95

Tragic Magic: Compromising Magical Sketches and a Number of Original Tricks, by Harry Leat. ISBN 1-59016-860-7 • 122 pages • illustrated • GB£8.95 • US$12.95

Tricks with Cards, by Professor Hoffman. ISBN 1-59016-866-6 • 145 pages • illustrated • GB£9.95 • US$13.95

Tricks and Magic Made Easy, by Edward Summers Squier. ISBN 1-59016- 867-4 • 188 pages • illustrated • GB£11.95 • US$15.95

Trix and Chatter, by W. Dornfeld. ISBN 1-59016-864-X • 286 pages • illustrated • GB£15.95 • US$21.95

Twenty Magical Novelties, by Bagshawe. ISBN 1-59016-875-5 • 80 pages • illustrated • GB£7.95 • US$11.95

Folklore and Mythology

Book of Rustem: Retold From the Shah Nameh of Firdausi, by E.M. Wilmot-Buxon. ISBN 1-59016-077-0 • 240 + xii + 10 illustrated pages • illustrated • GB£13.95 • US$19.95

Classic Myth-Lore in Rhyme, by Cary Blair McKenzie. ISBN 1-59016-125-4 • 104 + ii pages • illustrated • GB£7.95 • US$11.95

Classic Myths in English Literature and in Art: Volume One, by Charles Mills Gayley. ISBN 1-59016-126-2 • 276 + xxxxiv + 10 illustrated pages • illustrated • GB£17.95 • US$23.95

Classic Myths in English Literature and in Art: Volume Two, by Charles Mills Gayley. ISBN 1-59016- 127-0 • 319 + iv + 7 illustrated pages • illustrated • GB£17.95 • US$23.95

Dictionary of Mythology: Of Characters Found in Grecian and Roman Mythology, by John H. Bechtel. ISBN 1-59016-167-X • 221 pages • illustrated • GB£12.95 • US$17.95

Folk Tales from the Far East, by Charles H. Meeker. ISBN 1-59016-251-X • 254 + xii pages • illustrated • GB£14.95 • US$19.95

Fridthjof's Saga: A Norse Romance, by Esaias Tegnér. Translated from Swedish. ISBN 1-59016-257-9 • 213 + viii pages • GB£15.95 • US$12.95

Forty Modern Fables, by George Ade. ISBN 1-59016-253-6 • 303 + viii pages • GB£16.95 • US$22.95

Greek and Roman Mythology, by Jessie M. Tatlock. ISBN 1-59016-292-7 • 370 + xxxiv pages • heavily illustrated • GB£20.95 • US$26.95

On The Track of Ulysses, by W. J. Stillman. ISBN 1-59016-611-6 • 106 + xii pages • illustrated • GB£8.95 • US$12.95

Pan and His Pipes and Other Tales for Children, by Katherine Dunlap Cather. ISBN 1-59016-635-3 • 84 pages • illustrated • GB£7.95 • US$11.95

Stories of Norse Gods and Heroes, by Annie Klinggensmith. ISBN 1-59016-782-1 • 101 + ii pages • illustrated • GB£7.95 • US$11.95

The Student's Mythology, by C. A. White. ISBN 1-59016-814-3 • 315 + iv pages • GB£16.95 • US$22.95

Wine, Women and Song, by John Addington Symonds. ISBN 1-59016-918-2 • 180 + viii pages • GB£11.95 • US$15.95

The Young Folk's Book of Myths, by Amy Cruse. ISBN 1-59016-965-4 • 265 + xiv + 42 illustrated pages • heavily illustrated • GB£16.95 • US$22.95

Archaeology

The Romance of Excavation, by David Masters. ISBN 1-59016-736-8 • 191 + xiv + 25 illustrated pages • illustrated • GB£12.95 • US$17.95

Archaeology of the Delaware River Valley, by Max Schrabisch. ISBN 1-59016-037-1 • 181 + viii pages • illustrated • GB£11.95 • US$16.95

Magic Spades, by R. V. D. Magoffin and Emily C. Davis. ISBN 1-59016-504-7 • 348 + xiv pages • illustrated • GB£18.95 • US$24.95

The Stone, Bronze and Iron Ages, by John Hunter-Duvar. ISBN 1-59016-778-3 • 285 +xvi pages • illustrated • GB£15.95 • US$21.95

Sussex Archaeological Collections, compiled by the Sussex Archaeological Society. ISBN 1-59016-819-4 • 215 + vi + 16 illustrated pages • illustrated • GB£13.95 • US$18.95

Ancient History

The Biblical Story of Creation, by Giorgio Bartoli. ISBN 1-59016-064-9 • 155 + iv + 2 illustrated pages • illustrated • GB£9.95 • US$14.95

A Brief History of Ancient Times, by James Henry Breasted. ISBN 1-59016-083-5 • 320 pages • illustrated • GB£16.95 • US$22.95

Darius the Great: Ancient Ruler of the Persian Empire, by Jacob Abbott. ISBN 1-59016-152-1 • 286 pages • illustrated • GB£15.95 • US$20.95

The Dawn of History: An Introduction to Pre-Historic Study. Edited by Charles Francis Keary. ISBN 1-59016-155-6 • 240 + viii pages • illustrated • GB£13.95 • US$18.95

An Ancient History for Beginners, by George Willis Botsford. ISBN 1-59016-029-0 • 492 + xxii + 36 maps/illustrated pages • illustrated • GB£25.95 • US$34.95

Heroes and Crises of Early Hebrew History, by Charles Foster Kent. ISBN 1-59016-309-5 • 251 + xvi pages • GB£14.95 • US$19.95

Outposts of Civilization, by W. A. Chalfant. ISBN 1-59016-623-X • 193 pages • GB£11.95 • US$16.95

Rasselas: Prince of Abyssinia, by Samuel Johnson. ISBN 1-59016-704-X • 263 + iv pages • GB£14.95 • US$19.95

Stories from the Early World, by R. M. Fleming. ISBN 1-59016-779-1 • 162 + xii + 11 illustrated pages • illustrated • GB£11.95 • US$15.95

The Upanishads: Translated into English with a Preamble and Arguments by G.R.S. Mead and Jagadisha Chandra Chattopadhyaya ISBN 1-59016-883-6 • 137 pages • illustrated • GB£9.95 • US$13.95

Mesopotamian Religion

Assyria: Its Princes, Priests and People, by Archibald Henry Sayce. ISBN 1-59016-047-9 • 166 pages • illustrated • GB£10.95 • US$14.95

The Religion of Babylonia and Assyria, by Theophilus G. Pinches. ISBN 1-59016-708-2 • 126 pages • illustrated • GB£8.95 • US$13.95

Religious and Moral Ideas in Babylonia and Assyria, by Samuel A. B. Mercer. ISBN 1-59016-711-2 • 129 + xiv pages • illustrated • GB£9.95 • US$13.95

Mesopotamian History

Ancient Assyria, by C. H. W. Johns. ISBN 1-59016-025-8 • 175 + 2 illustrated pages • illustrated • GB£10.95 • US$15.95

Ancient Babylonia, by C. H. W. Johns. ISBN 1-59016-026-6 • 148 pages • illustrated • GB£9.95 • US$14.95

The Ancient Empires of the East, by Archibald Henry Sayce. ISBN 1-59016-032-0 • 303 + xxiv illustrated pages • illustrated • GB£16.95 • US$23.95

Babylonian Life and History, by Ernest Alfred Thompson Wallis Budge. ISBN 1-59016-054-1 • 168 pages • illustrated • GB£10.95 • US$15.95

Book of History: Volume IV, The Middle East: India, Ceylon, Burma, Siam and Central Asia, by W. M. Flinders Petrie, et al. ISBN 1-59016-074-6 • 434 + vi pages • illustrated • GB£21.95 • US$28.95

The Civilization of Babylonia and Assyria: Volume One, by Morris Jastrow, Jr. ISBN 1-59016-120-3 • 236 + xx + 31 illustrated pages • illustrated • GB£15.95 • US$21.95

The Civilization of Babylonia and Assyria: Volume Two, by Morris Jastrow, Jr. ISBN 1-59016-121-1 • 277 + xx + 45 illustrated pages • illustrated • GB£17.95 • US$23.95

History of Babylonia, by George Smith. ISBN 1-59016-320-6 • 192 pages • illustrated • GB£11.95 • US$16.95

History of Babylonia and Assyria, by Hugo Winkler. ISBN 1-59016-321-4 • 352 + xii pages • illustrated • GB£18.95 • US$24.95

A History of Babylonia and Assyria: Volume One, by Robert William Rogers. ISBN 1-59016-316-8 • 429 + xx + 2 illustrated pages • illustrated • GB£21.95 • US$29.95

A History of Babylonia and Assyria: Volume Two, by Robert William Rogers. ISBN 1-59016-317-6 • 418 + xvii pages • illustrated • GB£21.95 • US$28.95

History of Egypt, Chaldea, Syria, Babylonia and Assyria: Volume Six, by Gaston Maspero. ISBN 1-59016-324-9 • 446 + xiv pages • illustrated • GB£22.95 • US$29.95

Life in Ancient Egypt and Assyria, by Sir Gaston Camille Charles Maspero. ISBN 1-59016-463-6 • 374 +xviii pages • illustrated • GB£19.95 • US$26.95

Mesopotamia: The Babylonian and Assyrian Civilization, by L. Delaporte. ISBN 1-59016-516-0 • 369 + xxii pages • illustrated • GB£19.95 • US$26.95

Mesopotamian Archaeology, by Percy S. P. Handcock. ISBN 1-59016-518-7 • 421 + xxii + 31 illustrated pages • illustrated • GB£22.95 • US$30.95

Myths and Legends of Babylonia and Assyria, by Lewis Spence. ISBN 1-59016-547-0 • 410 + 22 illustrated pages • illustrated • GB£21.95 • US$28.95

Popular Dictionary of Assyrian and Babylonian Terminology, by F. C. Norton. ISBN 1-59016-655-8 • 201 pages • illustrated • GB£11.95 • US$16.95

A Smaller Ancient History of the East, by Philip Smith. ISBN 1-59016-766-X • 316 pages • illustrated • GB£16.95 • US$22.95

Stories of Ancient Peoples, by Emma J. Arnold. ISBN 1-59016-784-8 • 232 + ii illustrated pages • illustrated • GB£13.95 • US$18.95

The Story of Chaldea, by Zénaïde A. Ragozin. ISBN 1-59016-787-2 • 381 + xxii pages • 56 illustrations • GB£20.95 • US$26.95

The Story of Extinct Civilizations of the East by Robert E. Anderson. ISBN 1-59016-790-2 • 213 pages • illustrated • GB£12.95 • US$17.95

The Sumerians: A Civilization in 3,500 B.C., by C. Leonard Woolley. ISBN 1-59016-818-6 • 198 + x + 24 illustrated pages • illustrated • GB£12.95 • US$18.95

Voices of the Past: From Assyria and Babylonia, by Henry S. Roberton. ISBN 1-59016-892-5 • 219 + 24 illustrated pages • illustrated • GB£14.95 • US$19.95

Translations from the Past

Armenian Literature, with a Special Introduction by Robert Arnot. ISBN 1-59016-038-X • 142 + x + 1 illustrated pages • illustrated • GB£9.95 • US$14.95

Assyrian and Babylonian Literature, with Critical Introduction by Robert Francis Harper. ISBN 1-59016-044-4 • 480 + lxxxxvi + 4 illustrated pages • illustrated • GB£26.95 • US$35.95

Babylonian Literature, with a Special Introduction by Epiphanius Wilson. ISBN 1-59016-055-X • 309 + viii + 3 illustrated pages • illustrated • GB£16.95 • US$22.95

Egyptian History

Ancient Egypt From the Records, by M. E. Monckton Jones. ISBN 1-59016-028-2 • 244 + x + 13 illustrated pages • illustrated • GB£14.95 • US$19.95

Egyptian History and Art, by A. A. Quibell. ISBN 1-59016-203-X • 178 + xii + 15 illustrated pages • illustrated • GB£11.95 • US$16.95

Egyptians of Long Ago, by Louise Mohr. ISBN 1-59016-204-8 • 154 pages • illustrated • GB£9.95 • US$14.95

An Excursion in the Levant: 1903 by Colonel Thomas Innes. ISBN 1-59016-222-6 • 82 + 31 illustrated pages • illustrated • GB£8.95 • US$12.95

Kings and Gods of Egypt, by Alexandre Moret. ISBN 1-59016-438-5 • 290 + xii + 16 illustrated pages • illustrated • GB£16.95 • US$22.95

Our Inheritance in the Great Pyramid: Volume One, by Piazzi Smyth. ISBN 1-59016-614-0 • 296 + xviii + 23 illustrated pages • illustrated • GB£17.95 • US$23.95

Our Inheritance in the Great Pyramid: Volume Two, by Piazzi Smyth. ISBN 1-59016-615-9 • 328 + vi pages • illustrated • GB£17.95 • US$23.95

Tutankhamen and the Discovery of his Tomb, by G. Elliot Smith. ISBN 1-59016-870-4 • 133 pages • illustrated • GB£8.95 • US$13.95

Greek History

Epochs of Ancient History: The Greeks and The Persians, by G. W. Cox. ISBN 1-59016-214-5 • 218 + xxii + 4 illustrated pages • illustrated • GB£13.95 • US$18.95

Greek Architecture and Sculpture, by T. Roger Smith and George Redford. ISBN 1-59016-294-3 • 145 pages • illustrated • GB£9.95 • US$13.95

Greek Tragedy, by J. T. Sheppard. ISBN 1-59016-296-X • 160 + viii pages • illustrated • GB£10.95 • US$14.95

The Heroes or Greek Fairy Tales, by Charles Kingsley. ISBN 1-59016-310-9 • 208 pages • GB£10.95 • US$15.95

History of the Sciences in Greco-Roman Antiquity, by Arnold Reymond. ISBN 1-59016-330-3 • 245 + x pages • illustrated • GB£13.95 • US$19.95

Old Greek Life, by J. P. Mahaffy. ISBN 1-59016-596-9 • 101 pages • illustrated • GB£7.95 • US$11.95

Pompeii: Its Life and Art, by August Mau. ISBN 1-59016-652-3 • 558 + xxii + 18 illustrated pages • illustrated • GB£26.95 • US$35.95

The Story of the Greeks, by H. A. Guerber. ISBN 1-59016-804-6 • 288 pages • illustrated • GB£15.95 • US$21.95

Roman History

History of Nero, by Jacob Abbott. ISBN 1-59016-328-1 • 321 pages • 12 illustrations • GB£16.95 • US$22.95

Ancient Rome: From The Earliest Times Down to 476 A.D. compiled by R. F. Pennell. ISBN 1-59016-031-2 • 206 + iv pages • illustrated • GB£12.95 • US$17.95

Historical Tales: Roman Times, by Charles Morris. ISBN 1-59016-312-5 • 340 + ii + 11 illustrated pages • illustrated • GB£18.95 • US$24.95

An Introduction to Roman History Literature and Antiquities, by A. Petrie. ISBN 1-59016-370-2 • 126 pages • illustrated • GB£8.95 • US$12.95

Rambles in Rome, by S. Russell Forbes. ISBN 1-59016-702-3 • 368 + xxx pages • illustrated • GB£20.95 • US$26.95

A Short History of Rome and Italy, by Mary Platt Parmele. ISBN 1-59016-763-5 • 276 + xvi pages • GB£15.95 • US$21.95

Stories in Stone from the Roman Forum, by Isabel Lovell. ISBN 1-59016-781-3 • 258 + x + 14 illustrated pages • illustrated • GB£15.95 • US$20.95

History of the Americas

America Not Discovered by Columbus, by Rasmus B. Anderson. ISBN 1-59016-018-5 • 164 pages • illustrated • GB£10.95 • US$14.95

The Story of Extinct Civilizations of the West, by Robert E. Anderson. ISBN 1-59016-791-0 • 195 pages • illustrated • GB£11.95 • US$16.95

Ancient Civilizations of Mexico and Central America, by Herbert J. Spinden. ISBN 1-59016-027-4 • 270 pages • illustrated • GB£14.95 • US$20.95

Aztecs and Mayas, by Thomas J. Diven. ISBN 1-59016-049-5 • 248 pages • illustrated • GB£13.95 • US$19.95

Discoveries of America to 1525, by Arthur James Weise. ISBN 1-59016-170-X • 378 + xiv + 21 illustrated pages • illustrated • GB£20.95 • US$27.95

History of Latin America, by Hutton Webster. ISBN 1-59016-326-5 • 243 + xiv + 36 illustrated pages • GB£15.95 • US$21.95

The Spanish Conquerors, by Irving Berdine Richman. ISBN 1-59016-771-6 • 238 + iv pages • GB£13.95 • US$18.95

The Story of the Panama Canal, by Logan Marshall. ISBN 1-59016-808-9 • 286 + 72 illustrated pages • illustrated • GB£18.95 • US$24.95

American History

The Constitution of the United States: A Historical Survey of Its Formation, by Robert Livingston Schuyler. ISBN 1-59016-141-6 • 211 + viii pages • GB£12.95 • US$17.95

Historic Shrines of America, by John T. Faris. ISBN 1-59016-314-1 • 419 + 40 illustrated pages • GB£21.95 • US$29.95

History of California, by Helen Elliott Bandini. ISBN 1-59016-323-0 • 302 pages • GB£15.95 • US$21.95

The History of the United States, by John Clark Ridpath. ISBN 1-59016-332-X • 218 + viii + 9 illustrated pages • illustrated • GB£13.95 • US$18.95

One Hundred Years of the Monroe Doctrine, by Robert Glass Cleland. ISBN 1-59016-607-8 • 127 pages • GB£8.95 • US$12.95

The Southern Mountaineers, by Samuel Tyndale Wilson. ISBN 1-59016-770-8 • 202 + xiv pages • GB£12.95 • US$17.95

The Story of the Constitution, prepared by Sol Bloo. ISBN 1-59016-802-X • 192 pages • illustrated • GB£11.95 • US$16.95

The Transformation of Job: A Tale of the High Sierras, by Frederick Vining Fisher. ISBN 1-59016-865-8 • 214 + xviii pages • heavily illustrated • GB£13.95 • US$18.95

The War Myth in the United States, by C. H. Hamlin. ISBN 1-59016-902-6 • 92 + iv pages • GB£7.95 • US$11.95

European History

The Great Historians, by Kenneth Bell and G. M. Morgan. ISBN 1-59016-288-9 • 349 + viii pages • GB£18.95 • US$24.95

A Primer of Heraldry for Americans, by Edward S. Holden. ISBN 1-59016-676-0 • 106 + x + 24 illustrated pages • illustrated • GB£9.95 • US$13.95

The Quest of the Colonial, by Robert and Elizabeth Shackleton. ISBN 1-59016-691-4 • 443 + xv pages • illustrated • GB£21.95 • US$28.95

Ten Frenchmen of the Nineteenth Century, by F. M. Warren. ISBN 1-59016-832-1 • 265 + vi + 9 illustrated pages • illustrated • GB£15.95 • US$20.95

General History

Epochs of Modern History, by William Stubbs. ISBN 1-59016-215-3 • 300 + viii + 2 illustrated pages • illustrated • GB£16.95 • US$22.95

Ice Ages: The Story of the Earth's Revolutions, by Joseph McCabe. ISBN 1-59016-352-4 • 134 + x + 4 illustrated pages • illustrated • GB£9.95 • US$14.95

The Lost Cities of Ceylon, G. E. Mitton. ISBN 1-59016-482-2 • 256 + xiv + 34 illustrated pages • illustrated • GB£15.95 • US$21.95

The Revolutionary Spirit Preceding the French Revolution, by Félix Rocquain. ISBN 1-59016- 717-1 • 186 + xii pages • GB£11.95 • US$16.95

World History

Henry VIII and His Court, Herbert Beerbohm Tree. ISBN 1-59016-308-7 • 117 + vi pages • illustrated • GB£8.95 • US$12.95

Eventful Dates in the History of the World, by Felix Berol. ISBN 1-59016-220-X • 176 pages • GB£11.95 • US$15.95

The Fifteen Decisive Battles of the World: From Marathon to Waterloo, by E. S. Creasy. ISBN 1-59016-238-2 • 364 pages • GB£18.95 • US$24.95

The World's Revolutions, by Ernest Untermann. ISBN 1-59016-933-6 • 176 + ii pages • GB£10.95 • US$15.95

Medieval History

Tales of the Crusaders, by Anonymous. ISBN 1-59016-829-1 • 327 pages • illustrated • GB£17.95 • US$23.95

Scottish Chiefs: The Life Story of Sir William Wallace, by Jane Porter. ISBN 1-59016-758-9 • 350 + iv pages • illustrated • GB£18.95 • US$24.95

The Holy Grail: Six Kindred Addresses and Essays, by James A. B. Scherer. ISBN 1-59016-338-9 • 210 pages • GB£11.95 • US$16.95

King Arthur and His Knights, by Maude L. Radford. ISBN 1-59016-435-0 • 268 pages • illustrated • GB£14.95 • US$19.95

King Arthur and the Knights of the Round Table, by Charles Morris. ISBN 1-59016-436-9 • 255 + vi + 5 illustrated pages • illustrated • GB£14.95 • US$19.95

A Syllabus of Medieval History, by Dana Carleton Munro and George Clarke Sellery. ISBN 1-59016-824-0 • 148 + viii + (42 + iv) pages • GB£11.95 • US$16.95

Anthropology

Peasants & Potters, by Harold Peake and Herbert John Fleure. ISBN 1-59016-644-2 • 152 + vi pages • illustrated • GB£10.95 • US$14.95

The Chain of Life, by Lucretia Perry Osborn. ISBN 1-59016-112-2 • 189 + xiv + 14 illustrated pages • illustrated • GB£12.95 • US$17.95

The Fruit of the Family Tree by Albert Edward Wiggam. ISBN 1-59016-262-5 • 389 + xiv pages • GB£20.95 • US$26.95

Our Prehistoric Ancestors, by Herdman Fitzgerald Cleland. ISBN 1-59016-618-3 • 377 + xii pages • illustrated • GB£19.95 • US$26.95

Prehistoric Man, by Joseph McCabe. ISBN 1-59016-670-1 • 128 + vi + 6 illustrated pages • illustrated • GB£9.95 • US$13.95

The Rise of Man, by Paul Carus. ISBN 1-59016-728-7 • 103 + vi pages • illustrated • GB£8.95 • US$12.95

The Story of Ab, by Stanely Waterloo. ISBN 1-59016-786-4 • 292 + viii pages • GB£15.95 • US$21.95

The Story of Mankind, by Hendrik Van Loon. ISBN 1-59016-795-3 • 488 + xxxii + 8 illustrated pages • heavily illustrated • GB£24.95 • US$32.95

Paleontology and Prehistoric World

Animals of the Past, by Frederic A. Lucas. ISBN 1-59016-034-7 • 207 + xii pages • illustrated • GB£12.95 • US$17.95

Prehistoric Sussex, by E. Cecil Curwen. ISBN 1-59016-671-X • 172 + x + 31 illustrated pages • illustrated • GB£12.95 • US$17.95

Stories of the Universe: The Earth in Past Ages, by H. G. Seeley. ISBN 1-59016-783-X • 190 pages • illustrated • GB£11.95 • US$17.95

Story of Language

The Story of the Alphabet, by Edward Clodd. ISBN 1-59016-800-3 • 209 pages • illustrated • GB£12.95 • US$17.95

The Life and Growth of Language, by William Dwight Whitney. ISBN 1-59016-461-X • 327 + x pages • illustrated • GB£17.95 • US$23.95

The Science of Etymology, by Walter W. Skeat. ISBN 1-59016-756-2 • 242 + xx pages • GB£14.95 • US$19.95

Writing and Authorship

Writing the Short Story, by Joseph Berg Esenwein. ISBN 1-59016-942-5 • 441 + xvi pages • illustrated • GB£22.95 • US$29.95

Brief Business English and Business Letters, by Benjamin J. Campbell and Bruce L. Vass. ISBN 1-59016-084-3 • 192 + viii pages • GB£11.95 • US$16.95

The Century Handbook of Writing, by Garland Greever and Easley S. Jones. ISBN 1-59016-110-6 • 228 + xiv pages • GB£13.95 • US$18.95

Elementary Composition and Rhetoric, by William Edward Mead. ISBN 1-59016-209-9 • 286 pages • GB£15.95 • US$20.95

The Hand Book of Conversation: Its Faults and Graces, compiled by Andrew P. Peabody. ISBN 1-59016-302-8 • 152 pages • GB£9.95 • US$14.95

The Preparation of Manuscripts for the Printer, by Frank H. Vizetelly. ISBN 1-59016-673-6 • 148 + vi pages • illustrated • GB£9.95 • US$14.95

Technical Writing, by T. A. Richard. ISBN 1-59016-831-3 • 178 + vi pages • GB£10.95 • US$15.95

Acting and Cinematography

A Condensed Course in Motion Picture Photography, by the New York Institute of Photography. ISBN 1-59016-139-4 • 382 + 100 illustrated pages • illustrated • GB£22.95 • US$30.95

Film Folk, by Rob Wagner. ISBN 1-59016-241-2 • 356 + x pages • illustrated • GB£19.95 • US$26.95

Screen Acting: Its Requirements and Rewards, by Inez and Helen Klumph. ISBN 1-59016-760-0 • 243 pages • illustrated • GB£13.95 • $18.95

The Art of Make-Up, by Helena Chalmers. ISBN 1-59016-039-8 • 159 + viii pages • illustrated • GB£10.95 • US$14.95

Stage Scenery and Lighting, by Samuel Seldon and Hunton D. Sellman. ISBN 1-59016-772-4 • 433 + xiv pages • illustrated • GB£22.95 • US$29.95

Theater and Drama

The Art of Play Production, by John Dolman, Jr. ISBN 1-59016-040-1 • 464 + xviii + 12 illustrated page • illustrated • GB£22.95 • US$30.95

British Drama, by Allardyce Nicoll. ISBN 1-59016086-X • 496+ viii + 16 illustrated pages • illustrated • GB£24.95 • US$32.95

The Comic Spirit in Restoration Drama, by Anonymous. ISBN 1-59016-133-5 • 148 + viii pages • GB£9.95 • US$14.95

The Development of the Drama, by Branders Matthews. ISBN 1-59016-163-7 • 351 + vi pages • GB£18.95 • US$24.95

Drama and Mankind, by Halcott Glover. ISBN 1-59016- 180-7 • 192 pages • GB£11.95 • US$16.95

The Drama: Its Law and Its Technique, by Elisabeth Woodbridge. ISBN 1-59016-181-5 • 181 + xvi pages • GB£11.95 • US$16.95

Historic Costume, by Katherine Morris Lester. ISBN 1-59016-313-3 • 244 pages • illustrated • GB£13.95 • US$18.95

How to Produce Plays and PagEants, by Mary M. Russell. ISBN 1-59016-346-X • 219 + 10 illustrated pages • illustrated • GB£12.95 • US$17.95

On The Art of the Theatre, by Edward Gordon. ISBN 1-59016-610-8 • 296 + xxii + 14 illustrated pages • illustrated • GB£17.95 • US$23.95

The Popular Theatre, by George Jean Nathan. ISBN 1-59016-657-4 • 236 pages • GB£13.95 • US$18.95

Rhythmic Action Plays and Dances, by Irene E. Phillips Moses. ISBN 1-59016-722-8 • 164 + vi pages • illustrated • GB£10.95 • US$15.95

Scenes and Machines of the English Stage During the Renaissance, by Lily B. Campbell. ISBN 1-59016-751-1 • 302 + x + 8 illustrated pages • illustrated • GB£169.95 • US$22.95

The Story of the Theater, by Glenn Hughes. ISBN 1-59016-809-7 • 421 + x + 28 illustrated pages • illustrated • GB£22.95 • US$29.95

Studies in Stagecraft, by Clayton Hamilton. ISBN 1-59016-815-1 • 298 + vi pages • GB£15.95 • US$21.95

Theatron: An Illustrated Record of Twentieth Century Theater, by Clarence Stratton. ISBN 1-59016-838-0 • 260 + ii pages • illustrated • GB£16.95 • US$22.95

The Twentieth Century Theatre, by William Lyon Phelps. ISBN 1-59016-873-9 • 147 + vi pages • GB£9.95 • US$14.95

Science and Technology

The ABCs of Wireless Radio, by Edward Trevert. ISBN 1-59016-004-5 • 116 pages • illustrated • GB£8.95 • US$12.95

The Einstein Theory of Relativity, by Garrett P. Serviss. ISBN 1-59016-207-2 • 108 pages • illustrated • GB£7.95 • US$11.95

ABCs of the Telephone, by James E Homans. ISBN 1-59016-002-9 • 347 + xxiv pages • illustrated • GB£19.95 • US$25.95

The Age of Invention, by Holland Thompson. ISBN 1-59016-012-6 • 267 + x pages • GB£14.95 • US$20.95

Dreams of an Astronomer, by Camille Flammarion. ISBN 1-59016-187-4 • 223 pages • GB£12.95 • US$17.95

Elements of General Science, by Otis William Caldwell and William Lewis Eikenberry. ISBN 1-59016-210-2 • 402 + xviii pages • illustrated • GB£20.95 • US$27.95

The Fairyland of Science, by Arabella B. Buckley. ISBN 1-59016-228-5 • 266 pages • illustrated • GB£15.95 • US$19.95

A Laboratory Manual in Physics, by N. Henry Black. ISBN 1-59016-451-2 • 115 + x pages • illustrated • GB£8.95 • US$12.95

Maker's of Progress, by William L. and Stella H. Nida. ISBN 1-59016-506-3 • 208 + vi pages • illustrated • GB£12.95 • US$17.95

Marvels of Modern Mechanics, by Harold T. Wilkins. ISBN 1-59016-508-X • 280 + xii + 15 illustrated pages • illustrated • GB£16.95 • US$22.95

Telsa, Nikola: Various Articles, Patents and Lectures - Coming Soon, Call 1 (800) 952-LOST for our current catalog.

Nineteenth Century Photography: Anthony's Annual International Photographic Bulletin, June 1891. ISBN 1-59016-569-1 • 468 + xxii + 14 illustrated pages • illustrated • GB£24.95 • US$32.95

Principles of Bacteriology, by Arthur A. Eisenberg. ISBN 1-59016-678-7 • 198 pages • illustrated • GB£11.95 • US$16.95

Robinson's Manual of Radio Telegraphy and Telephony, by Captain S. S. Robinson, U.S. Navy. ISBN 1-59016-732-5 • 307 + vi illustrated pages • illustrated • GB£16.95 • US$22.95

Steam, Steel and Electricity, by James W. Steele. ISBN 1-59016-777-5 • 240 + viii pages • illustrated • GB£13.95 • US$18.95

The Story of Invention, by Hendrik Van Loon. ISBN 1-59016-793-7 • 252 pages • heavily illustrated • GB£13.95 • US$19.95

The Story of the Art of Building, by P. Leslie Waterhouse. ISBN 1-59016-801-1 • 215 pages • illustrated • GB£12.95 • US$17.95

The Wonders of Science in Modern Life, by Henry Smith Williams and Edward H. Williams. ISBN 1-59016-922-0 • 191 + viii + 8 illustrated pages • illustrated • GB£11.95 • US$16.95

Games, Entertainment, Humor

The American Checker Player's Hand Book, by Erroll A. Smith. ISBN 1-59016-020-7 • 160 pages • illustrated • GB£9.95 • US$14.95

Chess for Beginners, by E. E. Cunnington. ISBN 1-59016-114-9 • 112 pages • illustrated • GB£8.95 • US$12.95

A Comic History of the United States, by Livingston Hopkins. ISBN 1-59016-132-7 • 223 pages • illustrated • GB£12.95 • US$17.95

Common Sense in Chess, by Emanuel Lasker. ISBN 1-59016-136-X • 139 pages • illustrated • GB£9.95 • US$13.95

Dances, Drills and Story Plays: For Every Day and Holidays, by Nina B. Lamkin. ISBN 1-59016-151-3 • 117 pages • GB£8.95 • US$12.95

Dick's Games of Patience: Solitaire with Cards, edited by William B. Dick. ISBN 1-59016-166-1 • 154 + ii pages • GB£9.95 • US$14.95

Fun With Cards, by Dean Bryden. ISBN 1-59016-266-8 • 165 + viii pages • GB£10.95 • US$15.95

Fun with paper Folding, by William D. Murray and Francis J. Rigney. ISBN 1-59016-267-6 • 95 + ii pages • illustrated • GB£7.95 • US$11.95

Games for the Playground, Home, School and Gymnasium, by Jessie H. Bancroft. ISBN 1-59016-276-5 • 454 + viii + 22 illustrated pages • illustrated • GB£22.95 • US$30.95

The Gentlemen's Hand-Book on Poker, by Florence. ISBN 1-59016-278-1 • 195 + viii pages • illustrated • GB£11.95 • US$16.95

How to Play Chess, by E. E. Cunnington. ISBN 1-59016- 345-1 • 88 pages • GB£7.95 • US$11.95

Mr. Punch's After Dinner Stories, edited by J. A. Hammerton. ISBN 1-59016-683-3 • 192 + ii pages • illustrated • GB£11.95 • US$16.95

Songs for Little Children, composed and arranged by Eleanor Smith. ISBN 1-59016-769-4 • 213 + viii pages • illustrated with musical score • GB£12.95 • US$17.95

Craftwork and Hobbies

The Glazer's Clay Book and How to Use It, by E. L. Raes. ISBN 1-59016-285-4 • 137 + ii pages • tables • GB£9.95 • US$13.95

Home Tanning and Leather Making Guide, by Albert B. Farnham. ISBN 1-59016-340-0 • 176 pages • GB£10.95 • US$15.95

The Industrial Arts in Spain, by Juan F. Riaño. ISBN 1-59016-358-3 • 276 + vi pages • illustrated • GB£15.95 • US$20.95

Instructional Units in Wood Finishing, by R. A. McGee and Arthur G. Brown. ISBN 1-59016-363-X • 128 pages • illustrated • GB£8.95 • US$13.95

The Stamp Collector, by Stanely C. Johnson. ISBN 1-59016-775-9 • 317 + 31 illustrated pages • illustrated • GB£17.95 • US$24.95

Swoope's Lessons in Practical Electricity: Volume One, by Erich Hausmann. ISBN 1-59016-822-4 • 344 + xii pages • heavily illustrated • GB£18.95 • US$24.95

Swoope's Lessons in Practical Electricity: Volume Two, by Erich Hausmann. ISBN 1-59016-823-2 • 348 + x pages • heavily illustrated • GB£18.95 • US$24.95

Music Studies

Caruso and the Art of Singing, by Salvatore Fucito and Barnet J. Beyer. ISBN 1-59016-104-1 • 219 + x + 12 illustrated pages • illustrated • GB£13.95 • US$18.95

The Theory and Practice of Musical Form, by J. H. Cornell. ISBN 1-59016-836-4 • 214 + xviii pages • heavily illustrated • GB£14.95 • US$19.95

How to Listen to Music, by Henry Edward Krehbiel. ISBN 1-59016-344-3 • 361 + xiv pages • illustrated • GB£18.95 • US$24.95

Introductory to Music, by Thaddeus P. Giddings, Will Earhart, Ralph Baldwin and Elbridge Newton. ISBN 1-59016- 372-9 • 176 + ii pages • GB£10.95 • US$15.95

Lessons in Musical History, by John Comfort Fillmore. ISBN 1-59016-457-1 • 183 + xviii + 37 chronology pages • GB£13.95 • US$18.95

Listening Lessons in Music, by Agnes Moore Fryberger. ISBN 1-59016-468-7 • 264 + xiv pages • GB£14.95 • US$20.95

Music Club Programs from All Nations, by Arthur Elson. ISBN 1-59016-541-1 • 185 + x + 9 illustrated pages • illustrated • GB£11.95 • US$16.95

Musical Harmony Simplified, by F. H. Shepard. ISBN 1-59016-545-4 • 242 + viii pages • heavily illustrated • GB£13.95 • US$19.95

The New Educational Music Course, by James M. McLaughlin. ISBN 1-59016-561-6 • 130 + viii pages • GB£9.95 • US$13.95

Outlines of Music History, by Clarence G. Hamilton. ISBN 1-59016-621-3 • 308 + xxxvi pages • illustrated • GB£17.95 • US$23.95

Practical Guide to the Ideal Home Music Library, by Albert E. Wier. ISBN 1-59016-662-0 • 113 + viii pages • illustrated • GB£8.95 • US$12.95

Standard History of Music, by James Francis Cooke. ISBN 1-59016-776-7 • 260 + ii pages • heavily illustrated • GB£18.95 • US$19.95

Song Books

Beeton's Book of Songs, edited by Ward, Lock & Co. ISBN 1-59016-059-2 • 162 + xiv pages • illustrated • GB£10.95 • US$15.95

From Song to Symphony, by Daniel Gregory Mason. ISBN 1-59016-259-5 • 243 + vi pages • illustrated • GB£13.95 • US$19.95

Glee and Chorus Book, by J. E. NeCollins. ISBN 1-59016-286-2 • 208 + ii pages • illustrated with musical score • GB£12.95 • US$17.95

The Ideal Home Music Library: Volume IX, Sentimental Music, compiled and edited by Albert E. Wier. ISBN 1-59016-355-9 • 256 + ii pages • illustrated with musical score • GB£14.95 • US$19.95

The Ideal Home Music Library: Volume X, Favorite Home Songs, compiled and edited by Albert E. Wier. ISBN 1-59016-356-7 • 336 + ii pages • illustrated with musical score • GB£17.95 • US$23.95

Junior Music, by Thaddeus P. Giddings, Will Earhart, Ralph L. Baldwin and Elbridge W. Newton. ISBN 1-59016-395-8 • 256 + ii pages • illustrated • GB£14.95 • US$19.95

Laurel Glee Book for Male Voices, by M. Teresa Armitage. ISBN 1-59016-455-5 • 126 + iv pages • illustrated with musical score • GB£8.95 • US$13.95

Our Familiar Songs and Their Authors: Volume One, by Helen Kendrick Johnson. ISBN 1-59016-612-4 • 290 + x pages • GB£15.95 • US$21.95

Our Familiar Songs and Their Authors: Volume Two, by Helen Kendrick Johnson. ISBN 1-59016-613-2 • 368 + viii pages • GB£18.95 • US$25.95

Song and Legend from the Middle Ages, selected and arranged by William D. McClintock and Porter Lander McClintock. ISBN 1-59016-767-8 • 141 + ii pages • GB£9.95 • US$13.95

Song Treasury: 20th Century Americana, compiled and edited by Harriet Garton Cartwright. ISBN 1-59016-768-6 • 214 + xviii pages • illustrated with musical score • GB£12.95 • US$18.95

Painting and Drawing

Aims and Ideals of Representative American Painters, written and arranged by John Rummell and E. M. Berlin. ISBN 1-59016-014-2 • 114 pages • GB£8.95 • US$12.95

Anatomy and Drawing, by Victor Perard. ISBN 1-59016-024-X • 175 + xx pages • illustrated • GB£11.95 • US$16.95

Applied Drawing, by Harold Haven Brown. ISBN 1-59016-036-3 • 266 + vi pages • illustrated • GB£14.95 • US$20.95

Art Studies for Schools, by Anna M. Von Rydingsvärd. ISBN 1-59016-043-6 • 185 + ii pages • heavily illustrated • GB£11.95 • US$15.95

Drawing Made Easy, by Joseph Cummings Chase. ISBN 1-59016-183-1 • 146 pages • GB£9.95 • US$13.95

Electrical Drafting and Design, by Calvin C. Bishop. ISBN 1-59016-208-0 • 165 + vi pages • illustrated • GB£10.95 • US$15.95

Letters and Lettering: A Treatise with Two Hundred Examples, by Frank Chouteau Brown. ISBN 1-59016-459-8 • 214 + xviii pages • heavily illustrated • GB£12.95 • US$18.95

Painters, Pictures and the People, by Eugene Neuhaus. ISBN 1-59016-631-0 • 224 + x + 31 illustrated pages • illustrated • GB£14.95 • US$19.95

Painting and Decorating Working Methods, produced under the direction of Painting and Decorating Contractors of America. ISBN 1-59016-633-7 • 294 + xiv pages • illustrated • GB£16.95 • US$22.95

The Practice of Oil Painting and of Drawing, by Solomon J. Soloman. ISBN 1-59016-667-1 • 278 pages • illustrated • GB£14.95 • US$20.95

The Story of Dutch Painting, by Charles H. Caffin. ISBN 1-59016-789-9 • 210 + viii + 31 illustrated pages • illustrated • GB£13.95 • US$19.95

The Story of French Painting, by Charles H. Caffin. ISBN 1-59016-792-9 • 232 + xii + 40 illustrated pages • illustrated • GB£15.95 • US$20.95

Topographical Maps and Sketch Mapping, by J. K. Finch. ISBN 1-59016-851-8 • 175 + xiv + 3 illustrated pages • heavily illustrated • GB£11.95 • US$16.95

Famous People

Abraham LincolN: Volume One, by Carl Sandburg. ISBN 1-59016-007-X • 298 + x pages • GB£16.95 • US$22.95

Abraham Lincoln: Volume Two, by Carl Sandburg. ISBN 1-59016-008-8 • 304 + ix pages • GB£16.95 • US$22.95

Benjamin Franklin: American Statesman, by John T. Morse, Jr. ISBN 1-59016-061-4 • 442 + xxii + 2 illustrated pages • illustrated • GB£22.95 • US$30.95

Celebrated Female Sovereigns, by Anna B. Jameson. ISBN 1-59016-109-2 • 245 pages • illustrated • GB£13.95 • US$18.95

Famous Women, by Joseph Adelman. ISBN 1-59016-231-5 • 328 + x pages • illustrated • GB£17.95 • US$23.95

The Life of Benjamin Franklin, by M. L. Weems. ISBN 1-59016-466-0 • 239 + 5 illustrated pages • illustrated • GB£13.95 • US$18.95

Macaulay's Life of Samuel Johnson, edited by Albert Perry Walker. ISBN 1-59016-501-2 • 92 + xxxii + 6 illustrated pages • illustrated • GB£8.95 • US$13.95

Memorable Addresses by American Patriots, from a collection by John Clark Ridpath. ISBN 1-59016-513-6 • 112 + ii pages • GB£8.95 • US$12.95

Messer Marco Polo, by Donn Byrne. ISBN 1-59016-521-7 • 147 + iv pages • GB£9.95 • US$14.95

The Pocket University: Famous Explorers, edited by George Iles. ISBN 1-59016-648-5 • 171 + x pages • GB£10.95 • US$15.95

Questions and Answers

Answer This One: Questions for Everyone, compiled by Franklin P. Adams and Harry Hansen. ISBN 1-59016-035-5 • 192 pages • illustrated • GB£11.95 • US$16.95

One Thousand and One Riddles, compiled by David McKay. ISBN 1-59016-609-4 • 203 + ix pages • GB£11.95 • US$16.95

The Question Book for Young Folks, compiled by Sylvia Weil and Rosetta C. Goldsmith. ISBN 1-59016-688-4 • 95 pages • illustrated • GB£7.95 • US$11.95

What's The Answer? edited by John A. Bassett. ISBN 1-59016-910-7 • 111 + iv pages • GB£8.95 • US$12.95

Geology and Minerals

Diamonds and Other Gems, by John Clyde Ferguson. ISBN 1-59016-164-5 • 160 pages • illustrated • GB£9.95 • US$14.95

The Tragedy of PelEe, by George Kennan. ISBN 1-59016-859-3 • 257 + 14 illustrated pages • illustrated • GB£14.95 • US$20.95

Field Book of Common Rocks and Minerals, by Frederic Brewster Loomis. ISBN 1-59016-236-6 • 278 + xvi + 73 illustrated pages • illustrated • GB£18.95 • US$24.95

A First Book in Geology, by N. S. Shaler. ISBN 1-59016-245-5 • 255 + xx pages • illustrated • GB£14.95 • US$20.95

Geographic Influences in American History, by Albert Perry Brigham. ISBN 1-59016-280-3 • 285 + x pages • illustrated • GB£15.95 • US$21.95

Geography of California, by Harold W. Fairbanks. ISBN 1-59016-281-1 • 239 + ii + 2 illustrated pages • illustrated • GB£13.95 • US$18.95

Mineral Tables for the Determination of Minerals by Their Physical Properties, by Arthur S. Eakle. ISBN 1-59016-522-5 • 73 + iv pages • tables • GB£7.95 • US$11.95

San Francisco's Great Disaster, by Anonymous. ISBN 1-59016-746-5 • 422 pages • heavily illustrated • GB£20.95 • US$27.95

Stories in Stone, by Willis T. Lee. ISBN 1-59016-780-5 • 226 + x + 49 illustrated pages • illustrated • GB£15.95 • US$21.95

Natural History

Marvels of Natural History, by Henry Davenport Northrop. ISBN 1-59016-509-8 • 360 + 12 illustrated pages • heavily illustrated • GB£18.95 • US$24.95

Nature's Program, by Gaylord Johnson. ISBN 1-59016-554-3 • 181 + vi pages • GB£11.95 • US$16.95

The Pocket University: The Earth Around Us, edited by George Iles. ISBN 1-59016-649-3 • 191 + xxii pages • GB£12.95 • US$17.95

Biology

Sex Secrets, by Robert B. Armitage, M.D. ISBN 1-59016- 761-9 • 317 + ii pages • heavily illustrated • GB£16.95 • US$22.95

The Sexual Life, by C. W. Malchow, M.D. ISBN 1-59016- 762-7 • 317 pages • GB£16.95 • US$22.95

Miscellaneous

The Art of Thinking, by Ernest Dimnet. ISBN 1-59016- 042-8 • 221 + xii pages • GB£13.95 • US$18.95

Character Reading Through Analysis of the Features, by Gerald Elton Fosbroke. ISBN 1-59016-113-0 • 193 + xii + 56 illustrated pages • heavily illustrated • GB£14.95 • US$19.95

Health and Nutrition

Strength From Eating, by Bernarr MacFadden. ISBN 1-59016-812-7 • 194 pages • illustrated • GB£11.95 • US$16.95

A Compend of Materia Medica and Therapeutics, by Samuel O. L. Potter. ISBN 1-59016-137-8 • 147 pages • GB£9.95 • US$13.95

Drug Encyclopedia, compiled by Brunswig Drug Company, circa 1908. ISBN 1-59016-190-4 • 241 pages • illustrated • GB£13.95 • US$18.95

Education and Schooling

College: What's the Use? by Herbert E. Hawkes. ISBN 1-59016-130-0 • 143 + vi pages • illustrated • GB£9.95 • US$14.95

A Junior Class History of the United States, by John J. Anderson. ISBN 1-59016-393-1 • 242 pages • illustrated • GB£13.95 • US$18.95

Poise: How to Attain It, by D. Starke. ISBN 1-59016-650-7 • 159 pages • illustrated • GB£9.95 • US$14.95

Coursework and Study Guides

A Course in Piloting Seamanship and Small Boat Handling, by Charles F. Chapman. ISBN 1-59016-144-0 • 120 pages • illustrated • GB£8.95 • US$12.95

A Course in Wood Turning, by Archie S. Milton and Otto K. Wohlers. ISBN 1-59016-145-9 • 200 pages • GB£11.95 • US$16.95

Money and Business

The Theory and History of Banking, by Charles F. Dunbar. ISBN 1-59016-835-6 • 199 + vi pages • illustrated • GB£11.95 • US$16.95

Money & Investments, by Montgomery Rollins. ISBN 1-59016-525-X • 493 + xxii + 22 misc pages • graphs • GB£24.95 • US$33.95

Patent Office Practice, by Archie R. McCrady. ISBN 1-59016-640-X • 385 + xx pages • illustrated • GB£20.95 • US$26.95

The Romance of Business, by W. Cameron Forbes. ISBN 1-59016-734-1 • 258 + viii + 3 illustrated pages • illustrated • GB£14.95 • US$20.95

Dictionaries and Reference

A Desk-Book of Idioms and Idiomatic Phrases, by Frank H. Vizetelly and Leander J. DeBekker. ISBN 1-59016-161-0 • 496 + x pages • GB£23.95 • US$31.95

The English Dictionarie of 1623, by Henry Cockeram. ISBN 1-59016-212-9 • 197 + xxii pages • GB£12.95 • US$17.95

Handy Dictionary of English Synonyms, by Thomas Fenby. ISBN 1-59016-305-2 • 268 + xii pages • GB£14.95 • US$20.95

A Handy Dictionary of Synonyms, by H. C. Faulkner. ISBN 1-59016-306-0 • 217 pages • GB£12.95 • US$17.95

The Nuttall Dictionary of Anagrams, A. R. Ball. ISBN 1-59016-584-5 • 120 pages • GB£8.95 • US$12.95

Practical Synonyms, by John H. Bechtel. ISBN 1-59016-664-7 • 226 + ii pages • GB£12.95 • US$17.95

Pronunciation Dictionary, by John H. Bechtel. ISBN 1-59016-680-9 • 143 + ii pages • GB£9.95 • US$13.95

The Reporter's Word Book, by Anonymous. ISBN 1-59016-715-5 • 155 + iv pages • GB£9.95 • US$14.95

The Story Key to Geographic Names, by O. D. Von Engeln and Jane McKelway Urquhart. ISBN 1-59016-785-6 • 279 + xiv pages • GB£15.95 • US$21.95

Words: Their Spelling, Pronunciation, Definition and Application, compiled by Rupert P. SoRelle and Charles W. Kitt. ISBN 1-59016-925-5 • 127 + ii pages • tables • GB£8.95 • US$13.95

The Writer's Bluebook, by Leigh H. Irvine. ISBN 1-59016-938-7 • 82 pages • GB£7.95 • US$11.95

Quotations

The Book of Familiar Quotations, compiled from Various Authors. ISBN 1-59016-070-3 • 503 + viii pages • GB£23.95 • US$32.95

The World's Best Epigrams, by J. Gilchrist Lawson. ISBN 1-59016-931-X • 231 pages • GB£12.95 • US$17.95

Books on Books

A Book for All Readers, by Ainsworth Rand Spofford. ISBN 1-59016-068-1 • 507 + vi pages • GB£24.95 • US$33.95

How To Form A Library, by H. B. Wheatley. ISBN 1-59016-343-5 • 248 + viii pages • GB£13.95 • US$18.95

The Story of Libraries and Book Collecting, by Ernest A. Savage. ISBN 1-59016-794-5 • 230 + vi pages • GB£13.95 • US$18.95

What I Know About Books, by George C. Lorimer. ISBN 1-59016-908-5 • 110 pages • GB£8.95 • US$12.95

Who Wrote It? by William A. Wheller. ISBN 1-59016- 915-8 • 174 + iv pages • illustrated • GB£10.95 • US$15.95

Novelty Books

The American Poets Birthday Book, by Various Poets. ISBN 1-59016-022-3 • 183 pages • illustrated • GB£11.95 • US$15.95

Beasley's Christmas Party, by Booth Tarkington. ISBN 1-59016-058-4 • 100 + iv pages • illustrated • GB£7.95 • US$11.95

A Campfire Girl's First Council Fire, by Jane L. Stewart. ISBN 1-59016-103-3 • 246 pages • illustrated • GB£13.95 • US$18.95

The Christmas Story From David Harum, by Edward Noyes Westcott. ISBN 1-59016-118-1 • 107 + x pages • GB£8.95 • US$12.95

Cupid's Cyclopedia, compiled by Oliver Herford and John Cecil Clay. ISBN 1-59016-148-3 • 100 pages • illustrated • GB£7.95 • US$11.95

Furniture and Decorating

Decorative Styles and Periods in the Home: Furnishings of the Nineteenth Century, by Helen Churchill Candee. ISBN 1-59016-159-9 • 297 + xx + 100 illustrated pages • illustrated • GB£20.95 • US$27.95

English Furniture of the Cabriole Period, by H. Avray Tipping. ISBN 1-59016-213-7 • 79 + vi + 32 illustrated pages • GB£8.95 • US$12.95

Furniture of the Nineteenth Century, compiled by the Century Furniture Company. ISBN 1-59016-270-6 • 156 pages • illustrated • GB£11.95 • US$14.95

Inside of One Hundred Homes, by William Martin Johnson. ISBN 1-59016-360-5 • 140 pages • illustrated • GB£9.95 • US$13.95

Inside the House of Good Taste, edited by Richardson Wright. ISBN 1-59016-361-3 • 155 + x pages • illustrated • GB£9.95 • US$10.95

Old Glass: European and American, by N. Hudson Moore. ISBN 1-59016-594-2 • 389 + xx pages • illustrated • GB£20.95 • US$27.95

Cooking and Household

Aunt Martha's Corner Cupboard: Stories about Tea, Coffee, Sugar and Rice, by Mary and Elizabeth Kirby. ISBN 1-59016-046-0 • 144 pages • 32 illustrations • GB£9.95 • US$14.95

Chafing Dish Possibilities, by Fannie Merritt Farmer. ISBN 1-59016-111-4 • 161 pages • GB£9.95 • US$14.95

One Hundred Tested Receipts, compiled by Jennie C. Benedict. ISBN 1-59016-606-X • 88 + ii pages • GB£7.95 • US$11.95

The Rumford Complete Cook Book, by Lily Haxworth Wallace. ISBN 1-59016-741-4 • 236 + xviii pages • GB£13.95 • US$19.95

The Saginaw Cook Book, compiled by the Women's Society of the First Congregational Church. ISBN 1-59016-744-9 • 247 + ii pages • GB£13.95 • US$19.95

The Skaneateles Cook Book, issued by the Women's Village Improvement Association. ISBN 1-59016-765-1 • 113 pages • GB£8.95 • US$12.95

The Tidioute Cook Book, compiled and arranged by Ladies from Tidioute, Pennsylvania. ISBN 1-59016-845-3 • 238 + ii pages • heavily illustrated • GB£13.95 • US$18.95

Children's Books

Children of History, by Mary S. Hancock. ISBN 1-59016-116-5 • 192 + ii pages • illustrated • GB£11.95 • US$16.95

Children's Sayings: Early Life at Home, by Caroline Hadley. ISBN 1-59016-117-3 • 160 pages • illustrated • GB£9.95 • US$14.95

Magic Stories, by Frank N. Freeman, Grace E. Storm, Eleanor M. Johnson and W. C. French. ISBN 1-59016-505-5 • 288 + ii pages • illustrated • GB£15.95 • US$21.95

Mother Hubbard's Melodies, with illustrations by Gordon Browne, R. Marriott Watson, L.L. Weedon and Others. ISBN 1-59016-527-6 • 146 + xiv pages • heavily illustrated • GB£9.95 • US$14.95

Top of the World Stories for Boys and Girls, by Emilie Poulsson and Laura E. Poulsson. ISBN 1-59016-850-X • 206 + ii + 15 illustrated pages • illustrated • GB£12.95 • US$17.95

Travel and Adventure

Adventures by Land and Sea, by Various Authors. ISBN 1-59016-010-X • 127 + x + 2 illustrated pages • illustrated • GB£9.95 • US$13.95

How the World Travels, by A. A. Methley. ISBN 1-59016- 342-7 • 127 + x + 2 illustrated pages • illustrated • GB£9.95 • US$13.95

Little Journeys to the Homes of Great Reformers, by Elbert Hubbard. ISBN 1-59016-472-5 • 170 + vi + 10 illustrated pages • illustrated • GB£11.95 • US$15.95

Scenes from Every Land, by Gilbert H. Grosvenor. ISBN 1-59016-753-8 • 216 pages • heavily illustrated • GB£12.95 • US$17.95

Sinbad and His Friends, by Simeon Strunsky. ISBN 1-59016-764-3 • 261 + viii pages • GB£14.95 • US$20.95

World Cruise of the Northern and Southern Hemispheres, by Thomas Cook & Son. ISBN 1-59016-928-X • 103 pages • illustrated • GB£7.95 • US$11.95

Short Stories

Among the Camps: Young People's Stories of the Civil War, by Thomas Nelson Page ISBN 1-59016-023-1 • 163 pages • illustrated • GB£10.95 • US$15.95

A Little Book of Profitable Tales, by Eugene Field. ISBN 1-59016-470-9 • 243 pages • illustrated • GB£13.95 • US$19.95

Sports and Athletics

Swimming Scientifically Taught: A Practical Manual for Young and Old, by Frank Eugen Dalton. ISBN 1-59016-943-3 • 247 pages • illustrated • GB£13.95 • US$18.95

Greek Athletics, by F. A. Wright. ISBN 1-59016-295-1 • 123 + 8 illustrated pages • illustrated • GB£9.95 • US$13.95

Physical Training Manual, by Sargent Arthur W. Wallander. ISBN 1-59016-646-9 • 159 pages • illustrated • GB£9.95 • US$14.95

Tumbling, Pyramid Building and Stunts for Men and Women, by Bonnie and Donnie Cotteral. ISBN 1-59016-868-2 • 143 + vi + 11 illustrated pages • illustrated • GB£9.95 • US$14.95

FBI Files Revealed

Einstein, Albert: FBI Files Revealed - Coming Soon, Call 1 (800) 952-LOST for our current catalog.

Tesla, Nikola: FBI Files Revealed. ISBN 1-59016-833-X • 276 pages • GB£14.95 • US$19.95

News and Information

NEXUS MAGAZINE is an international bi-monthly alternative news magazine, covering the fields of Suppressed Science, Earth's Ancient Past, Alternative Health, UFOs, the Unexplained and much more. For subscription information visit www.nexusmagazine.com or call 1 (888) 909-7474.

ATLANTIS RISING MAGAZINE: One of the best magazines on Atlantis, ancient mysteries, lost continents, cryptozoology, and a whole host of other related subjects. For subscription information visit www.atlantisrising.com or call 1 (800) 228-8381.

Steamshovel Press is a zine that is dedicated to exposing the secrets behind the conspiracies that have shaped history. For subscription information visit www.steamshovelpress.com

Paranoia – A Conspiracy Reader focuses on the more paranoid aspects of society. For subscription information visit www.paranoiamagazine.com

Flatland Magazine publishes a once-per-year zine that reviews the suppressed and secret evidence around us. Contact www.flatlandbooks.com or call 1 (707) 964-8326.

The Book Tree provides controversial and educational products to help awaken the public to new ideas and information that would otherwise not be available. For a free catalog visit www.thebooktree.com or call 1 (800) 700-TREE.

The International UFO Congress holds a twice-yearly, week long conference and film festival on UFOs and a variety of other subjects. People attend from around the world and it is considered the best conference of its kind. For additional information visit www.ufocongress.com or call 1 (303) 543-9443.

The Bay Area UFO Expo and Conference holds an annual conference in the fall each year. For information and a free program guide visit www.thebayareaufoexpo.com or call 1 (209) 836-4281.

Conspiracy Con holds it's conference on Memorial Day weekend each year. For information and a free program guide visit www.conspiracycon.com or call 1 (209) 832-0999.

Cosmic Connections conducts the **Earth Mysteries Conference** in the Fall and the **Crystal Healing Conference** in the Spring of each year. For more information visit www.chetsnow.com or call 1 (928) 204-1962.

The Bay Area Consciousness Network holds its annual conference in November each year. For information visit www.bacn.org

Adventures Unlimited holds its **World Explorers Club Ancient Mysteries Conference** several times a year. For more information or a program guide and a free book catalog visit www.wexclub.com or call 1 (815) 253-6390.

The **Northwest UFO Paranormal Conference** is held in the late spring each year. For more information visit www.seattlechatclub.org

The **Annual MUFON Symposium** is held every year in various locations. For a program guide or information on local chapters of MUFON visit www.mufon.com or call 1 (303) 932-7709.

The **Business Spirit Journal** produces several spiritual and consciousness-related conferences each year. For information visit www.bizspirit.com or call 1 (505) 474-7604.

The **Aztec UFO Symposium** is held once a year in the early spring in Aztec, NM, location of a famed UFO crash. For more information visit www.aztecufo.com or call 1 (505) 334-9890.

The **Alternate Realities Conference** (ARC) hold its annual conference in the Summer each year. For more information visit www.dreaman.org or call 1 (423) 735-0848.

The **Roswell UFO Odyssey** commemorates a UFO crash in New Mexico for the first week in July each year. For information visit www.uforoswell.com

Problems-Solutions-Innovations sponsors the **Controlled Remote Viewing** conference in the early summer each year. For more information visit www.crviewer.com

The 4th Annual **McMinnville UFO Fest** convenes in McMinnville, Oregon each year. For information visit www.ufofest.com or call 1 (503) 472-8427.

The International Remote Viewing Association holds its annual **Remote Viewing** conference once per year. For more information visit www.rvconference.org

The **Ancient of Days Conference** convenes in Rowell, NM each July 4th weekend.. For information visit www.ancientofdays.net or call 1 (505) 625-8496.

Controlled America hold several **conspiracy and mind control conferences** each year. For information visit www.controlledamerica.com

The American Psychotronics Association holds it annual conference in the midwest each year. For information visit www.psychotronics.org or call 1 (262) 742-4790.

The **Global Wings Conference** convenes in Colorado once per year in the Fall. For information visit www.global-wings.com

Join the **UFO Watch and Conference** in Hooper, Colorado each fall. For more information visit www.seekufos.com or call 1 (719) 378-2271.

The **Cancer Control Society** holds it annual conference in the fall each year in the Los Angeles area. This year's 31st annual conference is in Universal City. For more information visit www.cancercontrolsociety.com or call 1 (323) 663-7801.

The **Universal Light Expo** holds it's annual conference in the midwest each year. For more information visit www.universeexpo.com or call 1 (423) 735-0848.

The **American Massage Therapy Association** holds several conferences nationwide each year. For more information visit www.amtamassage.org or call 1 (847) 864-0123 x 143.

The **Integrity Research Institute** holds a free energy / new technology conference every year on the East coast. For more information visit www.integrityresearchinstitute.org

The **Body, Mind and Spirit Expo: Where America Explores the New Age** is an ongoing nationwide conference series. Coming to a city near you: Charlotte, NC; Virginia Beach, VA; Indianapolis, IN; Portland, OR; Phoenix, AZ; Long Beach, CA; Grand Rapids, WI; West Palm Beach, FL; Melbourne, FL; Orlando, FL; Van Nuys, CA; Atlanta, GA; Riverside, CA; Nashville, TN; Chicago, IL; San Mateo, CA; San Jose, CA; Raleigh, SC; Pasadena, CA; San Diego, CA; Kansas City, KS; Orange County, CA; Austin, TX; Houston, TX; New Orleans, LA; Seattle, WA; Richmond, VA; Greenboro, SC, Sacramento, CA; and many more. For more information visit www.bmse.net or call 1 (541) 482-3722. Please mention this ad.

The **Ozark UFO Conference** convenes each year in Kentucky. For information visit www.ozarkufo.iwarp.com or call 1 (501) 354-2558.

The **New Living Expo** is once twice a year in the San Francisco Bay Area. For information visit www.newlivingexpo.com or call 1 (415) 382-8300.

The **Conscious Living Expo** holds several conferences a year on the west coast. For additional information call 1 (888) 721-EXPO or visit www.consciouslivingexpo.com

Lost Arts Media produces a variety of **Ancient mysteries conferences** and **Travel programs** throughout the year. Come travel with like-minded and kindred friends. For information visit www.lostartsmedia.com or call 1 (800) 952-LOST.

Have Your Event Videotaped / Audiotaped and/or Listed Here Call 1 (800) 952-LOST or Visit www.lostartsmedia.com THANKS FOR BROWSING!!!

Printed in the United States
20708LVS00010B/16-18